T. S. Eliot's

The Waste Land

Other titles available in the series

Liz Bellamy
Jonathan Swift's Gulliver's Travels

Nicola Bradbury
Charles Dickens' Great Expectations

David Fuller
James Joyce's Ulysses

Pauline Nestor
Charlotte Bronte's Jane Eyre

Suzanne Raitt
Virginia Woolf's To the Lighthouse

Gene Ruoff
Jane Austen's Sense and Sensibility

David Seed
James Joyce's A Portrait of the Artist as a Young Man

T. R. Wright
George Eliot's Middlemarch

T. S. Eliot's
The Waste Land

Gareth Reeves
University of Durham

New York London Toronto Sydney Tokyo Singapore

First published 1994 by
Harvester Wheatsheaf
Campus 400, Maylands Avenue
Hemel Hempstead
Hertfordshire, HP2 7EZ

A division of
Simon & Schuster International Group

Typeset in 10½pt on 12 pt Sabon
by Keyboard Services, Luton

Printed and bound in Great Britain by
Biddles Ltd, Guildford and King's Lynn

British Library Cataloguing in Publication Data

A catalogue record for this book is available from the British Library

ISBN 0–7450–0738–4 (pbk)

1 2 3 4 5 98 97 96 95 94

Contents

Acknowledgements

I am grateful to the University of Durham for granting a period of research leave in which to work on this book, and to the staff of the University library for their help.

Throughout this book quotations from T. S. Eliot's poetry are from the 1963 edition of *Collected Poems 1909–1962*. As A. D. Moody has demonstrated, this is one of the two 'most nearly authoritative editions that we have' of the poetry (the other being *Collected Poems 1909–1935*). For a full account of the problems involved in establishing a definitive text, see Appendix A of Moody's *Thomas Stearns Eliot: Poet* (Cambridge: Cambridge UP, 1979).

Acknowledgement is made for permission to quote extracts from Eliot's works, as follows.

Eliot, reprinted by permission of Harcourt Brace Jovanovich, Inc., Mrs Valerie Eliot and Faber & Faber, Ltd.

From *The Letters of T. S. Eliot: Volume one, 1898–1922* edited by Valerie Eliot, reprinted by permission of Harcourt Brace Jovanovich, Inc., and Faber & Faber, Ltd.

Preface

The Waste Land has come to be regarded as one of the chief exemplars of modernism in English literature. But it appears to have earned this status more by accident than by design. Although Ezra Pound famously helped bring the poem into the world, it is doubtful that he understood the nature of the brainchild. Nor, it seems, did Eliot himself ever make up his mind about it. Does it express 'the plight of a whole generation', or is it 'a piece of rhythmical grumbling'? Is it a series of loosely connected fragments, 'thoughts of a dry brain in a dry season', or does it contain some principle of unity? Is it a vision of despair or a quest for salvation? For all the commentary and analysis it has attracted, it remains a riddle, and not only to its readers but also, as Maud Ellmann has remarked, to itself. The sense of resistance a reader experiences, even today, on encountering *The Waste Land* is essential to it. To get beyond that sense many critics have wanted to fix the poem, to find hidden narratives and plots. But by trying to familiarise ourselves with it we are in danger of wishing away its defining characteristics: its inscrutability, its distance, its very lack of familiarity.

A poem that is a riddle to itself must remain so: it can be elucidated but not paraphrased. Hence this study is based on the premise that *The Waste Land* needs close reading, although not in the spirit of the old New Criticism, which tended to work with assumptions about unity and closed form. Rather, my reading recognises that the poem is resolutely open-ended (and not merely floatingly 'indeterminate'), a view supported by recent developments in reader-response and reception theory. The poem enacts the sense of thought and feeling being discovered and developed at the moment of writing. Consequently every moment of the text deserves pondering. Its self-reflexivity mirrors self-scrutinising, locked-in, even solipsistic emotions. But within the poetry can also be felt the often thwarted attempt to break free into full-throated lyric utterance.

The allusiveness of *The Waste Land* has, notoriously, encouraged exegesis rather than criticism. If the present reading goes too far the other way, my excuse is that I wish to help correct the balance. To hear what the poem is up to I have found it necessary to begin at the beginning and work my way to the end. Otherwise there was the danger of erecting spurious structures. Allusive 'keys' are everywhere in the poem, but invariably one is left wondering if and how far the poem is undermining its own, and the reader's, pretensions. Madame Sosostris, for instance, intimates a host of clues, but who is she to be believed? *The Waste Land* remains, to this day, a very singular work. Its sense inheres, more than most poems in English, in the way it sounds (or, sometimes, does not sound, cannot be sounded). This reading, therefore, concentrates on all the ways of sounding: syntax, lineation, intonation.

I

Contexts

Historical and Cultural Context

Much of Eliot's poetry, and *The Waste Land* conspicuously, enacts a sense of displacement that remained with him always. He cultivated the role of exile; it became a carefully created identity, a self-protective cover. As an American living in England he sometimes signed himself 'metoikos', Greek for 'resident alien'.[1] He relished the in-between status, saying his poetry 'wouldn't be what it is if I'd been born in England, and it wouldn't be what it is if I'd stayed in America.'[2] But the American expatriate was only one version. He saw himself as exiled everywhere, in America, in France (after graduating from Harvard in 1910 he spent 'a romantic year' in Paris studying French literature, and philosophy, at the Sorbonne),[3] and even in what became his adopted country, Britain – as the following extract from a letter written when he was 40 testifies. Its writer stands outside himself, watching himself in the third person, while intimating what are for him some of the essential biographical facts:

> Some day I want to write an essay about the point of view of an American who wasn't an American, because he was born in the South and went to school in New England as a small boy with a nigger drawl, but who wasn't a southerner in the South because his people were northerners in a border state and looked down on all southerners and Virginians, and who so was never anything anywhere and who therefore felt himself to be more a

> Frenchman than an American and more an Englishman than a Frenchman and yet felt that the U.S.A. up to a hundred years ago was a family extension.[4]

'The point of view' is evidently unlocatable; and the voice's breathless forward movement conveys both displacement and a search for some place to rest.

In *The Waste Land* the sense of displacement has a wide historical and geographical context. Against the backdrop of the First World War and its aftermath, the rats and dead men, the talk of demobilisation, the vision of exploding cities, Jerusalem, Athens, Alexandria, Vienna, London, there are, for instance, the displaced aristocratic Marie and the 'hooded hordes' of 'swarming' refugees. The disintegration of European civilisation is the scenario for what comes across as a general sexual, moral and spiritual collapse. But does the poem's hallucinatory and phantasmagoric manner convey a state of mind more than a state of civilisation? Interior and exterior merge in a private world of sensation. As the next section will argue, this doubleness has been at the heart of critical debate about *The Waste Land* ever since its publication.

The war certainly affected Eliot personally, if indirectly. Jean Verdenal, his closest friend and intellectual companion during his year in Paris, was killed in the Dardanelles (Eliot dedicated his first volume of poetry, *Prufrock and Other Observations* [1917], to him); people close to his wife's family were killed fighting; her brother returned from the front to tell of mangled corpses and trench rats. But Eliot was characteristically wary of any trace of emotional indulgence. He looked askance at the war enthusiasm of those who, like his American relations, were at a safe distance. He wrote to his father:

> To me all this war *enthusiasm* seems a bit unreal, because of the mixture of motives. But I see the war partly through the eyes of men who have been and returned, and who view it, even when convinced of the rightness of the cause, in a very different way: as something very sordid and disagreeable which must be put through.'[5]

No doubt this authentic sense of the war's horror, and perhaps the consciousness of his inability to participate (he tried to enlist in the United States Naval Intelligence Service, but to no avail), gave personal urgency to the 'impersonal theory of poetry' promulgated in his essay 'Tradition and the Individual Talent' (1917), in which he tried to argue that great art is not expressive of the emotions of the individual: in another letter to his father he wrote that 'everyone's individual lives are so swallowed up in the one great tragedy, that one almost ceases to have personal experiences or emotions, and such as one has seem so unimportant!'[6]

Eliot's habitual way of keeping himself apart while appearing to belong, of being both alien and resident, is demonstrated by his wary association with the Bloomsbury Group at the time of *The Waste Land.* Consorting with Bertrand Russell and Leonard and Virginia Woolf, he was in touch with people who had inherited or earned status within Edwardian society and English culture. The group had many academic, literary and political connections. Yet they were also outsiders, unorthodox in their social and sexual behaviour and in their political leanings. Leonard Woolf was a determined anti-imperialist. Russell, an important philosopher of distinguished lineage, was a pacifist and a philanderer. Such views and behaviour were in many respects opposed to Eliot's. But Bloomsbury's position of nonconformity at the centre of the Establishment matched his powerful instinct for camouflage. In all this there was a strong element of self-preservation on Eliot's part, a remoteness that sought to go deeper, and more ruthlessly, than any social connections would allow. He wrote to Mary Hutchinson, also associated with the Bloomsbury Group through her friendship with Clive Bell:

> I like to feel that a writer is perfectly cool and detached, regarding other peoples' feelings or his own, like a God who has got beyond them; or a person who has dived very deep and comes up holding firmly some hitherto unseen submarine creature. But this sort of cold detachment is so *very* rare – and *stupid* detachment is so much the rule.[7]

The feeling here is akin to that behind the submarine imagery in *The Waste Land* ('Those are pearls that were his eyes. Look!', a line adapted from *The Tempest*: 'A current under sea / Picked his bones in whispers'). This letter was written in the year which saw the publication of 'Tradition and the Individual Talent', and it betrays, once again, the personal pressures behind the essay's impersonal theory, behind the 'cold detachment' of such sentences as 'The progress of an artist is a continual self-sacrifice, a continual extinction of personality.'[8]

This and similar sentiments in 'Tradition and the Individual Talent' strongly intimate a sense of relief at the 'extinction of personality'. But it is the burden of *The Waste Land* that though it would bury personal experiences and emotions, they re-emerge painfully and unexpectedly ('April is the cruellest month, breeding / Lilacs out of the dead ground'; 'Winter kept us warm, covering / Earth in forgetful snow'; 'What are the roots that clutch'; 'That corpse you planted last year in your garden, / Has it begun to sprout?'). One such experience is Eliot's unhappy marriage to the Englishwoman Vivien Haigh-Wood, who suffered from nervous mental and physical ailments. The marriage must have had some bearing on the sexual anxiety in the poem, although, as I argue in the section on 'Theoretical Perspectives' below, this should not lead to facile conclusions about Eliot's attitudes to women. Nor is it wise, as Peter Ackroyd warns, to find in *The Waste Land* an autobiographical transcription of their marriage. For instance, many readers identify Vivien with the woman in the neurasthenic episode of 'A Game of Chess' (lines 111–38). However, these lines must contain a large fictional component, otherwise Eliot would surely not have felt able to show her the poem in the making, which we know he must have done because she wrote in the margin of a draft of the episode 'WONDERFUL' and 'Yes & wonderful wonderful'.[9] Eliot's acute sexual inhibition and fear are revealed in several poems he wrote before the publication of *The Waste Land*. For instance, in the prose poem 'Hysteria', written in 1915, the speaker imagines himself swallowed by a *femme fatale*, 'lost finally in the dark caverns of her throat'. He is threatened by loss of identity, until, like the speaker at the end of *The Waste Land*, he takes refuge in salvageable 'fragments', and consciousness masters environment: 'I decided that if the shaking of her breasts could be stopped, some fragments of the afternoon might be collected, and I concentrated my attention with careful subtlety to this end.' In an obscure and allusive poem called 'Ode', published in 1920, apparently about a sexual *rite de passage*, the ritual is a failure: there is 'silence from the sacred wood', the 'Mephitic river' is 'uninspired', and Turnus's sombrely sonorous death at the end of the *Aeneid* is reduced to a disappointing sexual 'death', to what, in Lyndall Gordon's words, 'appears to be a premature ejaculation': 'Indignant / At the cheap extinction of his taking off.'[10] As can happen in *The Waste Land*, the poetry here takes refuge from, and thus signals, difficult emotions by switching into a disturbingly satirical register.

One of Eliot's poetic procedures for distancing himself from his emotions is his extensive and habitual art of allusion, by which personal experience can be seen from the perspective of other poets, other times. Dante's *Divine Comedy* provides one such perspective in *The Waste Land*; one memorable instance is the allusion to the *Inferno* in the hallucinatory crowd that flows over London Bridge at the end of 'The Burial of the Dead'. Other perspectives come from Conrad, John Day, Goldsmith, Kyd, Marvell, Middleton, Milton, Ovid, Shakespeare, Spenser, Verlaine, Virgil, Webster, to name some of the more apparent. But one of the most pervasive presences behind the poem is the great precursor of French Symbolist poetry, Charles Baudelaire, who showed Eliot a way to bring modern urban life into his poetry. Baudelaire's example is partly responsible for the phantasmagoric unreality of Eliot's *Waste Land* city. Eliot's note to the 'Unreal City' at the end of 'The Burial of the Dead' quotes the opening lines of Baudelaire's 'Les Sept Vieillards': 'Fourmillante cité, cité pleine de rêves, / Où le spectre, en plein jour, raccroche le passant!' (O swarming city, city full of dreams, / Where the ghost accosts the passer-by in broad daylight!).[11] The poem depicts a modern psychological Hades. Eliot learned from Arthur Symons's *The Symbolist Movement in Literature*, which he first read in 1908, how it is possible to turn outer circumstance, mundane 'reality', into the poet's interior and visionary world. For Baudelaire the exterior, material world can become a 'forest of symbols', transformed into images of the poet's inner life. The poet's psyche gets projected outwards 'as if a magic lantern threw the nerves in patterns on a screen', in the words of 'The Love Song of J. Alfred Prufrock' (1917). The poet thus stands outside his own emotions and feelings in order to observe them.

This process goes on in much of Eliot's pre-*Waste Land* poetry. The imagery of 'Rhapsody on a Windy Night' (1917), for instance, is a visible demonstration of the speaker's spiritual and emotional condition. 'Preludes' (1917) contains lines which can be read as commentary on this kind of poetic strategy:

> You dozed, and watched the night revealing
> The thousand sordid images
> Of which your soul was constituted;
> They flickered against the ceiling.

'Portrait of a Lady' (1917) creates drama out of the poet's emotions, and even as it does so acknowledges the slipperiness of self-expression: in Part III the speaker ironically stands back from his feelings to watch himself act them out:

> And I must borrow every changing shape
> To find expression . . . dance, dance
> Like a dancing bear,
> Cry like a parrot, chatter like an ape.
> Let us take the air, in a tobacco trance—

This is self-consciousness consciously arrived at, poetry that knows it is looking in the mirror, placing its emotions precisely.

The figure cut by some of these early poems was imitated from another nineteenth-century French poet, the Symbolist

Jules Laforgue, whose poetry makes a formally mannered virtue out of ironic self-regard. The speaker of 'The Love Song of J. Alfred Prufrock', for instance, comes partly out of Laforgue's dandyish, shape-changing persona. He can only 'find expression' through self-projection. He watches himself watching the world. Eliot's early poems watch themselves sometimes with sang-froid, as with the switch at the end of 'Preludes' from 'The notion of some infinitely gentle / Infinitely suffering thing' ('notion' sounds flickeringly ironic) to 'Wipe your hand across your mouth, and laugh', sometimes more elaborately, as with the Laforguian *dédoublement* of 'La Figlia Che Piange' (1917), whereby, as A. D. Moody explains, 'the poet assumes a double presence, being at once the actor and the consciousness of his action.' The action of this poem is both external and internal: 'The verbs at once declare [the girl's] actions and direct them.'[12] Consciousness directs the action on the stage of the mind according to desire, but at the end of the poem the speaker turns on himself with an insouciance like Laforgue's: 'Sometimes these cogitations still amaze / The troubled midnight and the noon's repose.' When in *The Waste Land* Eliot quotes the last line of Baudelaire's 'Au Lecteur', 'You! hypocrite lecteur! – mon semblable, – mon frère!', he implicates reader and poet in a conspiracy of self-conscious literariness that both confines and liberates.

To judge from his philosophical writings, Eliot was well aware of the emotional impulses behind the epistemology implicit in his poetry. The interest of his doctoral thesis, 'Experience and the Objects of Knowledge in the Philosophy of F. H. Bradley' (which he wrote as a philosophy graduate student of Harvard, completed in England in 1916, but was prevented by the war from submitting), lies less in its argument, which is expressed in an unapproachable style, as in what it reveals of Eliot's preoccupations and obsessions.[13] The thesis wants both to validate immediate experience and to reach beyond it. Peter Ackroyd describes the appeal to Eliot of Bradley's book *Appearance and Reality*:

> To combine scepticism with idealism, to recognize the limitations of ordinary knowledge and experience but yet to see that when they are organized into a coherent whole they might vouchsafe glimpses of absolute truth – there is balm here for one trapped in the world and yet seeking some other, invaded by sensations and yet wishing to understand and to order them.

Behind Eliot's thesis is an acknowledgement of painful solipsism. Immediate experience gained through what Bradley calls 'finite centres' is incomplete and even 'mad', but it is all that is valid for the individual: 'All significant truths are private truths.' But the thesis would somehow break out of solipsism: as Ackroyd writes,

> The purpose is to reach beyond the miasma of private experience and construct a world, or rather an interpretation of the world, 'as comprehensive and coherent as possible'. And so it is that throughout Eliot's work the idea of pattern or order becomes the informing principle.[14]

Hence 'Tradition and the Individual Talent', in denigrating the notion of the work of art as an expressive medium, elaborates its chemical analogy of the artistic process as a 'catalyst' which 'transforms' and 'fuses' the 'elements', the 'emotions and feelings' that enter its presence, into a new whole or pattern.[15] Hence also a statement such as this, from an essay by Eliot on another French Symbolist poet, Paul Valéry: 'not our feelings, but the pattern which we make of our feelings, is the centre of value.'[16] (The section on 'Theoretical Perspectives' will have more to say about these essays and Eliot's impersonal theory.)

> My external sensations are no less private to my self than are my thoughts or my feelings. In either case my experience falls within my own circle, a circle closed on the outside; . . . the whole world for each is peculiar and private to that soul.

Eliot quotes these words from Bradley's *Appearance and Reality* towards the end of his notes to *The Waste Land*, and his doing so attests to the solipsism from which he would free himself by trying to construct a pattern, the poem itself, out of and so beyond 'the miasma of private experience'. In the case of *The Waste Land*, 'making a pattern of the feelings' in order to 'extinguish the personality', as Eliot saw it, was, at its simplest, an editorial process of constructing a work out of lines, fragments and passages of poetry that had begun life at different times. Some of these attempts Eliot had started years earlier and abandoned, two of them (beginning '(Come in under the shadow of this red rock)' and 'A woman drew her long black hair out tight') at least as early as 1914.[17] There is therefore a self-reflexively literal meaning to the line near the end of *The Waste Land*, 'These fragments I have shored against my ruins': the poet assembles his fragments to compose his poem and also himself. The conscious mind deliberately manipulates what is thrown up by the unconscious.

An anxious marriage, the death in January 1919 of his father (whom Eliot was planning to visit in America and whom he had not seen for three and a half years), overwork as a teacher and then, less onerously, as an employee of the Colonial and Foreign Department at Lloyds Bank in the City of London, also reviewing, lecturing and writing criticism, all combined to precipitate in Eliot a nervous breakdown. He went first to the seaside town of Margate in Kent to rest ('On Margate sands. / I can connect / Nothing with nothing'), and then to Lausanne in Switzerland for treatment by an analyst. On the way to Lausanne he stopped off in Paris where he showed his friend and poetic mentor Ezra Pound the incomplete manuscript of what was to become *The Waste Land*; the final section, 'What the Thunder said', 'suddenly took shape and word' in Lausanne;[18] on his return to England he left Pound with the sheaf of drafts from which the final poem would emerge. Pound's 'Caesarian Operation' on the drafts is now legendary.[19] Years later Eliot was to remember the poem having been 'just as structureless, only in a more futile way, in the longer version'.[20] This is true, although Pound's cutting radically altered its balance and character. At some stage Eliot had considered the title 'He do the police in different voices', a quotation from Dickens's *Our Mutual Friend*; and indeed the original drafts did attempt a greater variety of styles and dramatic voices. The first section had been introduced by the comic monologue of a Boston-Irish rake, the third by a Popean pastiche about someone called Fresca, and the fourth by a seaman's narrative about a sea-voyage ending in shipwreck; Tiresias's monologue in Part III was condensed from a passage in quatrains rhyming *abab*; and there were many other smaller excisions and alterations (some of which will be discussed in the course of my reading of the text).[21] The original drafts read more like a *comédie humaine*, more a collection of poems than the concentrated emotional entity which is the finished work with its arresting contrasts and juxtapositions.

Pound's work on the drafts was extremely acute, but pragmatic; he cut out the otiose, the explanatory, the discursive, the merely bad. Ackroyd interestingly writes that 'Pound found [the poem's] very resistance to interpretation ... to be the key to its power.'[22] But, as Donald Davie argues with vigour, it is unlikely that Pound ever fully understood the nature of the poetry he so drastically edited. Pound, claims Davie, 'was a realist in a very old-fashioned sense', whereas Eliot was

> never far from the solipsism that lay behind the *symboliste* endeavour, one for whom the psychological reality of private torments took priority over any reality which announced itself as social and public. This difference between the two poets showed up in *The Waste Land* drafts. For among the rather few objections by Pound that Eliot paid no attention to were one or two which required him to make consistent, in terms of locality and historical period, some of his references to London life. Eliot seems to have ignored these suggestions because for him the physical and social landscape of London was no more than a screen on which to project a phantasmagoria that expressed his own personal disorders and desperations.[23]

Neither did Eliot himself, it seems, appreciate the nature of his brainchild in the months following its production. Even after Pound's extensive editorial work, Eliot was evidently still not convinced that *The Waste Land* cohered as a single entity, since he suggested that it might be published in parts over four issues of the American magazine *The Dial* (although in the event the magazine did publish it as one poem).[24] At one time he considered prefacing it with the poem 'Gerontion', no doubt to excuse, and imply a unitary consciousness for, the ensuing 'Thoughts of a dry brain in a dry season', the uncohering poetic fragments, as they then must have appeared to their author, that make up *The Waste Land*. What is now regarded as one of the chief exemplars of modernism came about, it appears, by chance.

Critical Reception

By contemporary standards of poetry sales, *The Waste Land*, though not a 'best-seller', sold well, and was especially popular amongst the avant-garde and Bloomsbury set. A comment of 1921, the year before *The Waste Land* came out, by the Bloomsbury art critic Clive Bell indicates the expectations Eliot's audience had of him and the kind of reception it was prepared to give his poem: 'Mr Eliot is about the best of our living poets, and, like Stravinsky, he is as much a product of the Jazz movement as so good an artist can be of any.'[1] The poem's first impact was as a work of iconoclastic brilliance among undergraduates and the younger generation of writers. During the interwar years it was highly influential as an image of the despair and disillusionment of the times. The 'Auden generation' of poets saw it as the great poem of postwar disintegration, and admired Eliot's ability to accommodate modern urban scenery. This was in spite of their disquiet, felt especially by Stephen Spender, at Eliot's right-wing politics. But Spender can still write, as late as 1992, about

> the visions of a dying culture in *The Waste Land* and *Ulysses*. For if we saw in these works witness of the decline of civilisation, we also saw them as assertions of the power of the poetic imagination to absorb the ruin of the time and to make new language out of it.'[2]

This reception runs counter to Eliot's reported estimation,

prominently displayed at the start of Valerie Eliot's edition of *The Waste Land* drafts:

> Various critics have done me the honour to interpret the poem in terms of criticism of the contemporary world, have considered it, indeed, as an important bit of social criticism. To me it was only the relief of a personal and wholly insignificant grouse against life; it is just a piece of rhythmical grumbling.[3]

These opposed reactions, reflecting *The Waste Land*'s double nature, set the terms for much of the critical debate: is the poem an interior world of private agony or an exterior world of urban despair, or are these in some way interdependent?

In the 1950s the influence of *The Waste Land* became less overwhelming, in part as a result of the 'Movement' poets' predilection for metrical regularity and a wariness of poetry that could not be accommodated to the demands of rationality (which is not to say that they wanted a poetry that went no further than the merely 'reasonable'). Thereafter its influence on poetic practice diminished markedly, as a result of attacks on two fronts. On the one hand, Eliot's kind of modernism began to be distinguished from Pound's at the expense of the former, especially in America.[4] On the other, in England a 'native' twentieth-century poetic tradition, from Thomas Hardy through Edward Thomas to Philip Larkin, was championed as an alternative to the modernist revolution of Pound and Eliot. But in recent years the influence of *The Waste Land* has once more been on the increase, and not merely as a result of the interest generated by the biographical studies of Lyndall Gordon and Peter Ackroyd in the life of a poet long associated with 'invisibility' and 'impersonality'.[5] In 1988 Seamus Heaney testified to the influence which C. K. Stead's book *The New Poetic* (1964) had on his appreciation of Eliot's poem:

> *The Waste Land* in Stead's reading is the vindication of a poetry of image, texture and suggestiveness; of inspiration; of poetry which writes itself. It represents a defeat of the will, an emergence of the ungainsayable and symbolically radiant out of the subconscious deeps. Rational structure has been overtaken

> or gone through like a sound barrier.... Stead thus rehabilitated Eliot as a Romantic poet.[6]

And in 1992 Ted Hughes published *A Dancer to God*, a book which sees Eliot as a great poet of consciousness and turns him into a shamanistic visionary who encompasses 'the spiritual tragedy of his epoch'.[7]

The publication of *The Waste Land* started a critical debate that continues to this day, although the terms in which it is now conducted are not quite the same. Early reviewers and critics, whether favourable or hostile, wrote about the poem in terms of 'theme', 'form' and 'content'. Some argued that it is formless and fragmented, that it lacks 'unity'. This could lead either to the charge that it is incoherent and obscure, that Eliot is not in control of his 'material', or to the defence that unprecedented conditions of chaos and disintegration demand unprecedented methods of poetic fragmentation – a defence that tries to maintain the categories of 'form' and 'content', which in their fragmented state continue to mirror each other. The adverse position was taken by Edgell Rickword in 1925, in a commentary that is perceptive in spite of his hostility to *The Waste Land*'s procedures: 'It is the danger of the aesthetic of *The Waste Land* that it tempts the poet to think the undeveloped theme a positive triumph and obscurity more precious than commonplace.' But he grants *The Waste Land* representative status: 'The apparently free, or subconsciously motivated, association of the elements of the poem allows that complexity of reaction which is essential to the poet now, when a stable emotional attitude seems a memory of historical grandeur.'[8] The favourable position was taken by Conrad Aiken in 1923: 'The poem succeeds – as it brilliantly does – by virtue of its incoherence, not of its plan; by virtue of its ambiguities, not of its explanations. Its incoherence is a virtue because its "donnée" is incoherence.'[9]

Other early reactions wanted to find unity in *The Waste Land*. In *A Survey of Modernist Poetry* (1927), a work more influential in its day than is now generally recognised, Laura Riding and Robert Graves argued that the poem, though long, has to be read with expectations suitable to 'a short poem: that is, as a unified whole. The reader can no more skip a passage in it than a line in a short poem and expect to understand the poem.'[10] Others argued that *The Waste Land* demands a new notion of formal unity, that the poem does cohere, but in ways new and difficult to define, though their presence can be felt. This was the position taken by Allen Tate in 1923 when defending the poem against John Crowe Ransom's strictures. Ransom's view was based on the Coleridgean notion of the unifying act of artistic creation: 'The mind of the artist is an integer, and the imaginative vision is a single act which fuses its elements'; but what *The Waste Land* offers in its place is merely disintegrative irony and parody.[11] In countering this argument Tate tried to redefine the concept of 'form': 'the "form" of *The Waste Land* is this ironic attitude which Mr. Ransom relegates to the circus'.[12] As Michael Grant points out, 'for Tate, it was precisely in the incongruities, labelled as "parody" by Ransom, that the "form" of *The Waste Land* resided, in the ironic attitude of the free consciousness that refused a closed system.' Grant goes on, 'For Ransom, there was, or should be, a "natural" cohesion between the form of the work and the order of things. . . . For Tate, the possibilities of such "natural" discourse were over.'[13]

Inseparable from the issue of formal unity is the question of the poem's centre of consciousness. This question has been raised from the beginning, either by implication or more directly. Eliot himself appears to have felt acutely uncertain about it, as his note on Tiresias betrays: 'the most important personage in the poem, uniting all the rest'. (See my reading of 'The Fire Sermon' for a more detailed account of Tiresias and Eliot's note.) In *New Bearings in English Poetry* (1932) F. R. Leavis accepted this note at face value, claiming that 'it provides the clue to *The Waste Land*. It indicates plainly enough what the poem is: an effort to focus an inclusive human consciousness.' The result is for Leavis a new kind of poetic coherence: 'The unity the poem aims at is that of an inclusive consciousness: the organization it achieves as a work of art... may, by analogy, be called musical. It exhibits no progression.'[14] This view anticipates Hugh Kenner's in *The Invisible Poet: T. S. Eliot* (1960), although Kenner dismisses Eliot's note on Tiresias as an attempt 'to supply the poem with a nameable point of view'. Instead, argues Kenner, what the poem presents is a 'zone of consciousness' in which perceived and perceiver are inseparable, and no personality is created detachable from the poem itself: 'The perceiver is describable only as the zone of consciousness where that which he perceives can coexist; but the perceived, conversely, can't be accorded independent status.'[15]

The manner of *The Waste Land*, in which inner and outer merge in the way Kenner describes, has made it notoriously difficult to pin down, to locate its centre of gravity. I. A. Richards wrote in 1926 that the poem expressed 'the plight of a whole generation'.[16] But Edmund Wilson was quick to question this view, wondering whether the malaise of *The Waste Land* is not personal, the subject for analysis being, not contemporary life, but Eliot's own temperament as projected on to civilisation:

> No artist has felt more keenly than Mr. Eliot the desperate condition of Europe since the War nor written about it more poignantly. Yet, as we find this mood of hopelessness and impotence eating into his poetry so deeply, we begin to wonder whether it is really the problems of European civilization which are keeping him awake nights. ... one suspects that his real significance is less that of a prophet of European disintegration than of a poet of the American Puritan temperament. ... the aesthetic and emotional waste land of the Puritan character.[17]

Edgell Rickword, too, in a review of *The Waste Land*, implied that its arena of action is internal as much as external: 'we seem to see a world, *or a mind*, in disaster, and mocking its despair' (my italics).[18]

Like much modernist writing, *The Waste Land* questions traditional notions of character as individual and stable. Like modernist writers such as James Joyce and Virginia Woolf, the

Eliot of *The Waste Land* experiments with forms of consciousness. Furthermore *The Waste Land* is by a poet who professed interest in the modernist practice of re-working myth and ritual. But if, as some have argued, Eliot was explaining the procedures of *The Waste Land*, to himself or to his readers, when formulating his celebrated 'mythical method' to describe *Ulysses*, I do not find that these sentences throw much light on his poem, whatever they do for Joyce's work:

> In using myth, in manipulating a continuous parallel between contemporaneity and antiquity, Mr. Joyce is pursuing a method which others must pursue after him.... It is simply a way of controlling, of ordering, of giving a shape and a significance to the immense panorama of futility and anarchy which is contemporary history.'[19]

The Waste Land may indeed succeed in 'giving a shape and a significance' to its author's sense of contemporary 'futility and anarchy', but it does not do so in Joyce's way. Attempts by critics to find 'continuous parallels' of this sort in *The Waste Land* end up ignoring the texture of the poem, that it is not in its nature to 'pursue' much 'method'. Its allusions come across as bricolage, fragments shored against the poet's ruins; and Robert L. Schwarz, for instance, is surely right to resist the schematic reading based on Jessie L. Weston's *From Ritual to Romance* and Frazer's *The Golden Bough*, a reading which 'not only distorts the poem but leaves incomplete the very understanding it seeks to promote'.[20]

For many years there have been readings that make *The Waste Land* into a spiritual quest. In part they are reacting against accounts of the poem as a vision of despair. They are likely to claim that the poem is the first step towards Christian belief, as, most notably, does Helen Gardner (1949),[21] and, acknowledging Gardner's influence, Lyndall Gordon, who writes in *Eliot's Early Years* (1977) that Eliot's poetry traces 'a consuming search for salvation'.[22] They can also enlist *The Waste Land* in the tradition of Western spirituality, as, most recently, does Eloise Knapp Hay in *T. S. Eliot's Negative Way* (1982).[23] Hay's argument is sophisticated: though Eliot's work from first to last does indeed evince a spiritual progression, it does not represent a steady development towards Christian belief. Although the 'negative way' is traceable in all Eliot's poems, before 1926 it is an indication of his philosophical scepticism; only later did it become transformed into the Christian *via negativa*. 'Too many readings have taken Eliot's early volumes and *The Waste Land* as poems already leading through death to the promise of new life', but, argues Hay, there is a decisive break between the poetry before and after Eliot's espousal of Anglo-Catholicism. This argument is a useful corrective, but it is in danger of replacing one inflexible schema by another. Hay claims that *The Waste Land*'s Christian allusions are negative; they are ironic presences indicating the absence of Christian belief. But against Hay it can be argued that the very act of negation is an acknowledgement of what is being denied. The text refuses the possibility of resolution. It is open-ended; but it is not indecisive. On the contrary, it is decided in its uncertainty. It patiently endures the prospect of inconclusion.

Theoretical Perspectives

The approach to *The Waste Land* indicated at the end of the previous section was taken by Frank Kermode in his article 'A Babylonish Dialect' (1967), in which he argued that the poem is an act of 'decreation' (a concept borrowed from Simone Weil). Against attempts to find order and coherence in *The Waste Land* can be set Kermode's statement: 'Eliot ridiculed the critics who found in *The Waste Land* an image of the age's despair, but he might equally have rejected the more recent Christian interpretations. The poem resists an imposed order.'[1] But this does not mean that readers will not continue to look for, and find, 'orders' in the poem; it discovers our hankering for coherence. And certainly there are plenty of coherences to be found: this is part of the difficulty, not that there are none but that they may be countless.

Thus the astonishing number and variety of readings of the poem have prompted critics in recent years to account theoretically for its apparently endless interpretability, to formulate a response to our responses. Attention has turned from describing the 'objective' characteristics of the text to defining its effects on the reader. Hence varieties of reader-response and reception theory have proved fruitful, in particular that of Wolfgang Iser, who argued that the critic should account for the effects of a text on the reader, rather than for its qualities as an object, because texts are by their nature receptive to many readings.[2] Steve Ellis has recently offered a thoughtful analysis based on Iser's ideas, concluding that there is a tug in *The Waste Land* between Eliot's 'undoubted sympathy with the subjectivism of readerly response' and his need 'for some kind of control'.[3] And Mick Burton has some perceptive things to say about the unstable relation between the reader and the text of *The Waste Land*.[4]

Hans-Georg Gadamer gives an important historical dimension to reader-response criticism, arguing, in Raman Selden's words, that 'the meaning of a text is not limited to the author's intentions but is continually extended by the later readings. . . . Any object we study can never be separated from our subjectivity.' Thus every reading 'becomes a focusing and ordering instrument in a complex perspective of horizons going right back to the contemporary reading of the text'.[5] This characterises the approach of Marianne Thormählen in *The Waste Land: A fragmentary wholeness* (1978). She takes Kermode's argument a stage further: 'Not only does *The Waste Land* resist an imposed order – it resists a limitation to any one interpretation.' Drawing support from J. Hillis Miller, she argues that it is in the nature of *The Waste Land* to need its reader and each act of reading to complete itself. Every interpretation is implicit, but each one is necessarily different from all others.[6] Her book combines an exhaustive survey of critical reactions to the text with her own synthetic perspective, thus attempting to get beyond limitation to a single interpretation.

Jewel Spears Brooker and Joseph Bentley, in their recent *Reading The Waste Land: Modernism and the limits of interpretation* (1990), see Eliot's modernist text as particularly susceptible to this kind of approach. Moreover, as they point out, Eliot himself, 'like Gadamer, ... saw interpretative activity as a never-ending process'. This is consonant with the fact that 'texts like *The Waste Land* present themselves primarily as linguistic structures. They tend to displace attention from the meaning of words to the meaning of meaning, from the end of interpretation to the process.' *The*

Waste Land is thus a highly self-reflexive text, demanding careful attention to the process of its unfolding, and Brooker and Bentley can justly claim that their analysis represents a long overdue 'return to close reading', an example which this study endorses and follows. Such an approach does not imply a return to the assumptions about unity and closed form implicit in the close readings of the New Critics with their ideals of objectivity and 'scientific' methodology:

> One problem with the work of the New Critics was that their close readings, no matter how brilliant, could not deliver all they seemed to promise. The emphasis on the text itself as a reservoir of meaning gave the impression that a text could be confronted and overcome through close reading, that questions could be answered in authoritative and final ways.[7]

Eliot's view of language, argue Brooker and Bentley, has much in common with that of Lévi-Strauss and Derrida: like them

> he saw every text as *bricolage* – work with tools known to be 'always already' fallen into imprecision. The hallmark of his major poetry is the use of language that is conscious of itself and of its finitude and thus is designed to put itself under erasure.[8]

This attitude to language derives in large part from French Symbolist aesthetics, which governed Eliot's poetic style at the time of *The Waste Land*, as Donald Davie demonstrates in his essays 'Mr Eliot' (1963) and 'Pound and Eliot: A Distinction' (1970).[9] Michael Grant usefully summarises:

> Donald Davie identified the crucial characteristic of Eliot's language as 'symboliste', in which, as in Mallarmé, language revealed itself, not as the expressive instrument of some individual or subject, but as pre-existing any user of it. The only 'events' in Eliot's poetry were the events of language, as words erupted into consciousness.... Eliot's poetry foregrounded its language, unlike the work of other poets, who justified their language by its referential content and who therefore regarded their language as transparent to realities beyond it. For Eliot... there was no such access to non-verbal reality, and none sought for.'[10]

It follows that in an account of *The Waste Land* talk of setting, plot, theme, character, is beside the point. Much of the critical exegesis of the poem, argues Davie, has been a waste of labour. We must attend to the action of the words. Denis Donoghue (1974) writes that in *The Waste Land* 'words are enforcing themselves as the only presences. What we respond to is the presence of the words.'[11]

The fact that over the course of his career Eliot wrote a number of essays about the French Symbolist poet Paul Valéry (with whom he was personally acquainted) testifies to the importance which the Symbolist aesthetic held for him. In 'A Brief Introduction to the Method of Paul Valéry' (1924) Eliot wrote that Valéry achieved 'an individual and *new* organisation of many poetic elements'.[12] Language for Valéry already contains 'elements' which are intrinsically 'poetic'; words are used not to express emotions and feelings, but for the emotions and feelings they already possess. This is language at an advanced stage of development, highly conscious of itself. Many years later Eliot wrote, in 'From Poe to Valéry' (1948), an essay that seems to sound his valediction to the Symbolist method: 'This process of increasing self-consciousness – or, as we may say, of increasing consciousness of language – has as its theoretical goal what we may call *la poésie pure*' (which is a sentence that self-consciously listens to itself: 'as we may say', 'what we may call'). This goal can never be achieved because a poem can never entirely dispense with subject matter without ceasing to be poetry. But with Valéry, argues Eliot, has come 'a change of attitude toward the subject matter. . . . it is important as *means*: the end is the *poem*. The subject exists for the poem, not the poem for the subject.' Eliot goes on to develop a theory about the 'combination' that takes place in the act of creation reminiscent of the chemical analogy of 'Tradition and the Individual Talent' (1917): 'A poem may employ several subjects, combining them in a particular way; and it may be meaningless to ask "What is the subject of the poem?" From the union of several subjects there appears, not another subject, but the poem.'[13] The opacity of the poem's language, its resistance to our seeing through it to an experience or situation outside the poem, throws the language and its surface effects into relief.

But it does not follow that, because *The Waste Land* is a highly self-conscious text, 'a major subject' of the poem 'is the contingency of language', as Brooker and Bentley claim. About most modernist texts it can be said that we are acutely conscious of 'the process of reading', but it does not follow that this is 'one of the poem's major subjects' either.[14] Although *The Waste Land*, like many other modernist works, may 'tend to displace attention ... from the end of interpretation to the process', this does not mean a reader should stop at the awareness of this process. That most modernist texts are self-reflexive makes it all the more important for the critic to penetrate beyond this defining characteristic. A text's procedure should not be confused with its subject matter.

Nor should *The Waste Land* be read as if it were simply an exemplar of Symbolism. The Symbolist aesthetic has itself been 'placed' by the poem. The aesthetic represents for Eliot an ideal against which the poem constantly tugs. It is indicative that behind a good many of Eliot's pronouncements about the nature of poetic language can be felt the pressure of personal emotions which he would anaesthetise. But the more he tries to escape expressivism, the tighter its hold. In 'A Brief Introduction to the Method of Paul Valéry' he writes:

> One is prepared for art when one has ceased to be interested in one's own emotions and experiences except as material; ... Valéry's interest in 'technique' is ... a recognition of the truth that not our feelings, but the pattern which we may make of our feelings, is the centre of value.[15]

The same repulsion and fascination in regard to the self informs 'Tradition and the Individual Talent': 'only those who have personality and emotions know what it means to want to escape from these things.'[16] In a deconstructive reading of Eliot in *The Poetics of Impersonality: T. S. Eliot and Ezra Pound* (1987), Maud Ellmann argues that his 'notion of impersonality is ... equivocal', and that his conception of 'a continual self-sacrifice, a continual extinction of personality', 'ennobles rather than degrades the poet' through its 'saintly renunciation of the self': 'the artist universalises his identity at the very moment that he seems to be negated.' The theory of impersonality does not deny 'subjectivism', but 'sets out to put the author *in his place*, and to liberate the poem from his narcissism'. 'Tradition and the Individual Talent' frequently strays into psychological terminology in spite of itself. It invites inspection of all that it wants to ward off. Ellmann writes that Eliot 'claims to be degrading authors into passive vehicles in which "emotions and feelings" may combine at will.... However, feelings presuppose a feeler. Eliot is attacking expressivism with its own weapons.'[17] Davie likewise argues that in 'Tradition and the Individual Talent' Eliot 'was groping for' a Mallarmean theory of poetry, in which 'it is language which happens through the speaker, not the speaker who expresses himself through language'; but 'instead of talking about impersonality as a poetic effect, a valuable illusion, he talked about the psychology of artistic creation.'[18] One symptom of Eliot's equivocation is the essay's uneasy shifting between '*im*personal' and '*de*personalised', as if the way to achieve impersonality in poetry were somehow to remove the personal flesh, leaving the impersonal skeleton standing pure and unemotional.

Eliot's prose writings thus betray a solipsism that would free itself from the feeling subject; and the same strain can be felt in *The Waste Land*. As Ellmann remarks, the poem is not only sphinx-like, luring the reader into exegetics when 'there is no secret underneath its hugger-mugger', it is also 'a riddle to *itself*'.[19] Symbolist poetry is based on a solipsistic aesthetic: 'what it says is always only itself', in Davie's words.[20] But *The Waste Land*'s solipsism is not merely a matter of aesthetics. The poem is acutely conscious of its locked-in feelings, and it would break free. Here is the emotional core of the poem, and it can be felt particularly in the thwarted attempts at full-throated lyric utterance. This is a poem concerned with more than 'the contingency of language'. The poetry would escape the trammels of self. The poet would be 'talking about himself without giving himself away', as Eliot was to remark many years later, supposedly about Virgil, but no doubt also about himself (thus giving himself away).[21]

Denis Donoghue writes that *The Waste Land* invites the reader

> to imagine a possible state of feeling which is secreted in the words. The best way to read the lines is not to ask that each phrase give up its meaning, as if that meaning were then to replace the words; but to ask what quality, in each sequence, the phrases share.[22]

That is a definition of *The Waste Land*'s kind of poetry, and a practical method of reading it. It is a method given exemplary demonstration in Christopher Ricks' *T. S. Eliot and Prejudice* (1988), a book exacting in the attention it pays to the self-reflexive workings of the poetry. Near the end Ricks quotes Eliot's remark, 'It isn't that I need time to make up my mind: I need time in order to know what I really feel at the moment.' Ricks goes on, 'This self-understanding is continuous with Eliot's understanding of art and of the nature of intelligence within art.'[23] *The Waste Land* enacts with self-aware patience the consciousness that it does not know what it really feels at the moment. This complicates our concluding anything about Eliot's prejudices: it is not that he did not possess them, but that his art is continually scrutinising them. This is one way of interpreting that statement by Eliot, 'not our feelings, but the pattern which we may make of our feelings, is the centre of value'. To take one important instance that has received a fair amount of attention in recent years: the question of misogyny in *The Waste Land*. The poem does not betray such feelings; it explores them.[24] Much of the evidence for Eliot as a misogynist comes from poetic drafts that never got as far as the final text, in particular the long passage about Fresca originally intended to open 'The Fire Sermon'.[25] But the critic has no right to read that passage, or any other, into the final text as if it had never been excised; due consideration must be given to why it was cut.[26] Nor is it enough, though, to cite as the sole motive for the excision Pound's comment that 'Pope has done this so well that you cannot do it better', for the questions remain, why did Eliot choose the Popean mode in the first place and why is it not right for what he thought he wanted to say?[27] Did the Fresca passage oversimplify complicated feelings to do with the poet's sexuality? Part of the burden of my reading is that *The Waste Land* wrestles in painful acknowledgement of those feelings. Central to the text is a recognition of women's suppression and violation, and, in keeping with its effort to attain (an impossible, so it seems to say) pure lyric poetry, it would give utterance to the strangulated but 'inviolable voice' of woman.

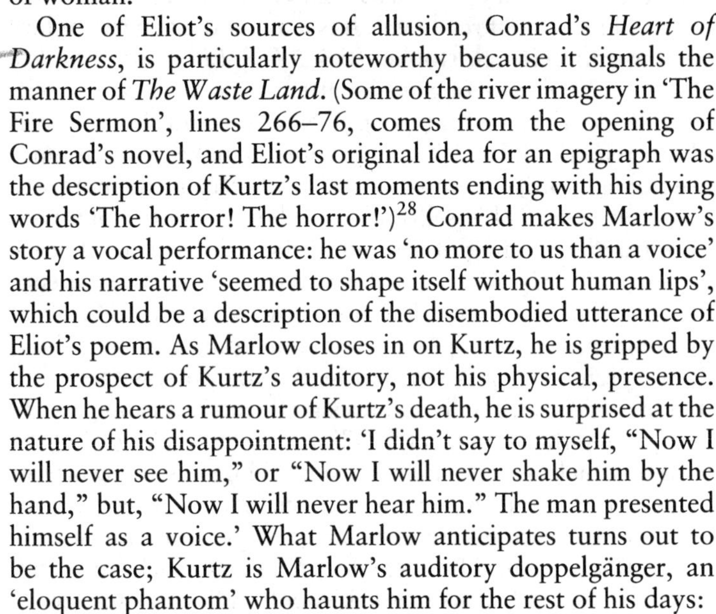

One of Eliot's sources of allusion, Conrad's *Heart of Darkness*, is particularly noteworthy because it signals the manner of *The Waste Land*. (Some of the river imagery in 'The Fire Sermon', lines 266–76, comes from the opening of Conrad's novel, and Eliot's original idea for an epigraph was the description of Kurtz's last moments ending with his dying words 'The horror! The horror!')[28] Conrad makes Marlow's story a vocal performance: he was 'no more to us than a voice' and his narrative 'seemed to shape itself without human lips', which could be a description of the disembodied utterance of Eliot's poem. As Marlow closes in on Kurtz, he is gripped by the prospect of Kurtz's auditory, not his physical, presence. When he hears a rumour of Kurtz's death, he is surprised at the nature of his disappointment: 'I didn't say to myself, "Now I will never see him," or "Now I will never shake him by the hand," but, "Now I will never hear him." The man presented himself as a voice.' What Marlow anticipates turns out to be the case; Kurtz is Marlow's auditory doppelgänger, an 'eloquent phantom' who haunts him for the rest of his days:

> And I was right, too. A voice. He was very little more than a voice. And I heard – him – it – this voice – other voices – all of them were so little more than voices – and the memory of that time itself lingers around me, impalpable, like a dying vibration of one immense jabber, silly, atrocious, sordid, savage, or simply mean, without any kind of sense.

At this point Marlow launches into a surrealistic reverie like

The Waste Land, in which chronology is disrupted and voices speak from the dead: 'You should have heard the disinterred body of Mr. Kurtz saying, "My Intended".' Kurtz can speak to Marlow in English, but we learn that 'All Europe contributed to the making of Kurtz'; and a polyglot congeries of European voices contributes to the making of *The Waste Land*.[29]

II

The Waste Land
A Reading of the Text

I

'The Burial of the Dead'

'The subject exists for the poem, not the poem for the subject.'[1] Eliot's statement confirms the sense of verbal self-consciousness with which *The Waste Land* opens. An ironising relationship is at once set up between reader and text; linguistic inflexion is paramount, as well as uncertain. The reader is engagingly disorientated. Christopher Ricks has described well how the 'force' of the opening words depends upon the combination of 'unmistakable direction' ('Manifestly the first five words are a disagreement with ... something which it is believed that you sentimentally believe') and the 'lurking possibilities of mistaking its direction', depending on whether you stress 'April', 'is', or 'cruellest': 'since the words are the very opening, we lack that sufficiency of established context which will often secure us.'[2] Hence some have heard the opening as sombrely impersonal, a prophetic voice out of the void, others as playful satire cocking a snook at time-worn notions of springtime awakening.

Yet early on the poem is surprisingly specific about the emotions it will involve. We might expect that the Eliot who professed an interest in the principles of 'imagism' would have avoided abstractions such as 'memory' and 'desire' this early in the poem, signalling what it might be 'about'. After all, had not Pound in his 'A Few Don'ts by An Imagiste' warned that the poet should 'Go in fear of abstractions'?[3] But to call 'memory' and 'desire' abstractions may be to fall into a trap, as Eliot knew:

> The confused distinction which exists in most heads between 'abstract' and 'concrete' is due not so much to a manifest fact of the existence of two types of mind, an abstract and a concrete, as to the existence of another type of mind, the verbal, or philosophic.[4]

The Waste Land's opening lines likewise warn against the trap, for they are quietly disturbing in the facility with which they 'mix' what are generally termed 'concrete' and 'abstract'. 'Breeding', 'land' and 'mixing' anticipate something physical, not the emotional abstractions of 'memory' and 'desire', words which thus become acutely involved with physical sensation. Conversely, the memory of or the desire for something can, painfully, turn what is remembered or desired into an abstraction. The blurring takes place in the word 'memory' itself, for it can mean both the thing remembered and the faculty of memory, concretion and abstraction. Memory can turn the thing remembered into an abstraction. Contrast the ending of 'The Burial of the Dead', where bringing memories back to life takes on a satirically sinister physical aspect: the 'corpse' of the past may 'sprout' and 'bloom'; it is dangerous to dig up the past ('O keep the Dog far hence, that's friend to men, / Or with his nails he'll dig it up again!').

The opening lines enact an emotional 'stirring' as the present participles twist and turn with desire at the end of their lines. The tug between wanting to forget and having to remember is enacted in the tug between syntax and line-breaks. 'Breeding', 'mixing', 'stirring', 'covering', 'feeding', five participles ending five of the poem's first six lines, each preceded by a caesura that breaks the line near its end, so that each participle is suspended: the effect is a repeated fading at the end of the line because of the weak syllable '-ing', a repeated stopping and starting again, a repeated anticipation of the next line, a repeated sagging and stiffening. The lines bestir themselves, repeatedly waking themselves out of a numbed forgetfulness, reluctantly complying in the impulse to remember. Torpor vies with activity. Memory transfixes while desire impels; or, memory released thaws the psyche while desire stymied paralyses it. Opposed emotions mix and stir. These opening lines display 'the nerves in patterns on a screen', in the words of 'The Love Song of J. Alfred Prufrock'. '[F]eeding / A little life with dried tubers' sounds metaphoric of the emotions as well as of the birthpangs of the poem itself. Compare and contrast the opening of *Four Quartets*, which talks ostentatiously in abstractions:

> What might have been is an abstraction
> Remaining a perpetual possibility
> Only in a world of speculation.

This is a deliberately abstract way of talking about the abstractions of memory and desire. It has been pointed out how one way of reading *Four Quartets* is as a conscious reworking of what had been going on in *The Waste Land* at a less conscious level.[5] The opening of *The Waste Land* does not talk about the mixing of memory and desire; it *goes* about it. The syntactic paralleling of the three phrases 'breeding / Lilacs out of the dead land', 'mixing / Memory and desire', 'stirring / Dull roots with spring rain', lessens the 'abstractness' of memory and desire, and makes them participate in the actions of the lilacs and the roots, which, however, resist turning into the 'dead' metaphor of the roots-of-memory variety.

Courting the dangers of such metaphor is a hallmark of Eliot's earlier poetry. His deployment of tropes that we loosely associate with Romantic poetry is an instance. 'The Love Song of J. Alfred Prufrock' begins with a 'pathetic fallacy' whose arch self-consciousness mingles absurdity with emotional acuity. The start of *The Waste Land* also deploys 'pathetic fallacy', with fewer shock tactics perhaps, but in a way that made Ezra Pound, for one, feel uncomfortable. He circled the word 'forgetful' in Eliot's draft, as if to question the ascription of human emotion to inanimate nature: cut the adjectival abstraction 'forgetful' and let the snow-covered earth perform its beguiling amnesia unaided.[6] Had not Pound's 'imagist' list of 'Don'ts' also warned poets to 'use no superfluous word, no adjective, which does not reveal something'?[7] But 'forgetful' stayed, unforgettably. It may not reveal anything about the snow, but it reveals something about the consciousness that thinks it.

Part of the reason for not being able to fix the attitude of the opening is the impossibility of identifying the speaker – or speakers, for the poem does not speak with a unitary voice even in the first verse-paragraph. At the start the poetry sounds disembodied, tending to the oracular, but towards the end of the paragraph it is embodied in hinted particularities of people, place, situation. If there is a change of speaker, it is from one that inclines to the impersonal to one that is full of personal circumstances, possibly Marie's. But where exactly does the change happen? If as early as line 5 (at 'Winter kept us warm'), the parallel phrasing, caesurae and lineation in the first seven lines carry the reader unsuspectingly from one voice into the other. If at line 8 (at 'Summer surprised us'), the phrases 'Winter kept us warm' and 'Summer surprised us' set up a counterpoint (winter did this, but summer did that) which carries us forward, again unsuspectingly, into that apparently personal narrative towards the end of the paragraph. And if there is a change of speaker at line 8, is the second 'us' (in 'Summer surprised us') different from or the same as the first (in 'Winter kept us warm')? As 'we' move via 'the colonnade' into the idyll, if that is what it is, of 'the Hofgarten', the lines move, with beguiling stealth, into a different, colloquial register, so that it is difficult to believe that the 'we' of 'Winter kept us warm', a phrase surrounded by elemental words ('roots', 'earth', 'life'), is the same as the 'we' who participate in the un-elemental activities of drinking coffee and talking for an hour.

Some hear the whole of the first verse-paragraph as spoken by Marie, which is just possible as long as one does not hear, as some have, any empty-headedness (which would not sound well with the oracular tendencies of the opening lines) in the fragmented reminiscence towards the end, with its clauses held together by 'and': 'And went on', 'And drank', 'and talked', 'And when we were children', 'And I was frightened', 'And down we went', 'and go south in the winter.' Do these repeating 'and' clauses signify naïve delight, wide-eyed and exclamatory, or a dulled sensibility? It is impossible to catch their intonation, or at any rate to fix on them any one intonation. 'In the mountains, there you feel free': B. C. Southam writes that 'in German, there is a romantic and somewhat clichéd expression with precisely this meaning', which might support the contention of empty-headedness.[8] On the other hand, the clipped phrasing of these lines may denote, not vacuousness, but upper-class laconism, with a touch of social vanity, the poised line-break in 'the arch-duke's, / My cousin's' hinting at the poise of social superiority – or of social insecurity. The lines may intimate the disintegration of postwar Europe, with Marie, a displaced central European, either recalling or inventing – depending on whether you hear fear of insecurity or nostalgia for a lost order – her erstwhile well-connected status: 'I am not Russian at all; I come from Lithuania; I am a real German.' But to translate the line of German is to make oneself deaf to its foreignness, to the fact that if this is the voice of one of the displaced, then it must go on sounding displaced. The line 'In the mountains, there you feel free' makes a 'dead sound', exhausted of vitality, denoting a sense of anything but a free spirit. 'I read, much of the night, and go south in the winter' sounds similarly listless.[9]

Displacement is the sensation frequently experienced by a reader trying to hear *The Waste Land*, written by an expatriate American with more knowledge about the past of his adopted Europe than many of its European inhabitants, and therefore less at home in it than if he had been ignorant of what it was he found lacking there. The opening paragraph enacts in microcosm the effect of the whole poem: the familiar-sounding, the clichéd even, displaced and made strange. 'In the mountains, there you feel free' sounds familiar, even if you do not know it is a translated German cliché. It sounds so well that it may in its turn be verging on a cliché in its English form; it may be that Marie, empty-headedly, is quoting something that she thinks sounds good. Similarly, 'I read, much of the night, and go south in the winter' sounds like a quotation, whether or not it is. The absence of quotation marks around the 'cousin's' words, which are evidently in direct quotation because Marie says they are ('He said, Marie, / Marie, hold on tight'), signals how, typically of *The Waste Land*, the opening paragraph releases language, from particular utterers, from intonational intention, from allusive contexts. Quotation, both direct speech and literary extract, floats free. Absence of quotation marks has the effect of levelling, or of raising, all the lines to the status of quotation. This is language listening to itself in the act of utterance. 'This process of increasing self-consciousness . . . has as its theoretical goal what we may call *la poésie pure*,' wrote Eliot.[10] 'Theoretical' to be sure: *la poésie pure* is certainly not attained in *The Waste Land*. But behind it sounds the hankering for that 'inviolable voice' (see 'A Game of Chess').

There is no consistency in this matter of quotation marks. The words of the 'cousin' are allowed to recede into the pattern of the poem. (It is only by means of what Marie remembers him as saying that we learn her name.) But this is not always so in 'The Burial of the Dead'. The words of the hyacinth girl are in quotation marks; so too are the words of the 'I' who addresses Stetson at the end. But Madame Sosostris's directly quoted words are not. Such arbitrariness warns against giving priority to any of the poem's voices.

Sometimes these voices come out of nowhere, as at the start of the second paragraph. This begins, like many other passages in *The Waste Land*, in what sounds like the manner of a set piece:

> What are the roots that clutch, what branches grow
> Out of this stony rubbish? Son of man,
> You cannot say, or guess, for you know only
> A heap of broken images

The manner of these lines is plainly oracular and prophetic. As Michael Edwards writes, they 'may be read as a description of the poem, and of the reader's problem'.[11] *The Waste Land* is attendant on its own birth-pangs, on its effort to make poetic sense out of the stonily intransigent material of memory. The advice Eliot received third-hand via Conrad Aiken, that to get over writer's block he should stop 'thinking he's God', made him 'speechless with rage' (even if it did, as Aiken surmises, 'do the trick'), but it may have found its prophetic Old Testament resonances in the poem that emerged.[12] Eliot's notes refer to Ezekiel and Ecclesiastes to elucidate the opening of the second paragraph. In Ezekiel 2: 1 it is God who says to the prophet 'Son of man' (He goes on, 'stand upon thy feet, and I will speak unto thee'), and there is something self-reflexively wry about Eliot making his poem take on the voice of God, as if in covert acknowledgement of the charge of hubris. Is the prophetic tone too audible for its own good? Does it ironically undermine its own pretensions? Is there an intimation of hollowness in these deep-sounding oracular sonorities, a deflating inflexion in the word 'rubbish', for instance and especially? 'Stony rubbish' does not have the same ring as 'broken images' or even as 'fragments shored'.

A large fragment Eliot had been shoring against his ruins for at least five years was a version of the six lines beginning at line 24 ('Only / There is shadow under this red rock'), originally the opening of the aborted poem 'The Death of Saint Narcissus'.[13] Christopher Ricks has made very high claims for these lines as they appear in *The Waste Land*, persuasively demonstrating their 'tonal power, welcoming and sinister, which is so fearfully inviting', an effect largely gained by the insertion of parentheses where there were none in the original version. He writes that they 'constitute one of Eliot's greatest triumphs, in their astonishing play of the cadences and the sense against the punctuation's demand'. He quotes these lines, omitting the one in parentheses,

> Only
> There is shadow under this red rock,
> And I will show you something different

and comments:

> The sense is so precarious as to sound deranged; a reader is therefore pressed to let the words '(Come in under the shadow of this red rock)' come in, or come out from the shadow of their brackets, in order that there may then be the sane sequence: 'Come in under the shadow ... And I will show you'. It is a revolutionary moment in English poetry, in the mildness of its violence, the intrepidity with which it realizes trepidation.[14]

The intrepidity and trepidation are partly at the prospect of the task being now performed and to be performed, the writing of *The Waste Land*. Even as the poet refashions one of the fragments from his heap of broken poetic images, he allows himself an intricacy of syntax that hardly squares with the declarativeness that goes with oracular authority.

The more one listens to the voice of this oracle, the more difficult it is to 'say' what it means or 'guess' at its insinuations. The small word 'only', for instance, equivocates, as it does elsewhere in *The Waste Land*.[15] '[F]or you know only / A heap of broken images' sounds either defeated or resolute, depending on whether 'only' means 'merely' or 'solely'. 'Only' is here suspended at the end of the line with fearful trepidation, as it is again three lines later with even more trepidation, since in the later instance it hesitates immediately after beginning a sentence: 'Only / There is shadow under this red rock'; here 'only' sounds as though it is about to offer the 'shelter' and 'relief' denied by 'dead tree', 'cricket' and 'dry stone'. But as we read on, the 'shadow' reveals an intenser fear, 'fear in a handful of dust'. These verbal suspensions suspend our emotions, draw out our anticipation, quiveringly holding open the possibility of either hope or despair, or rather 'the deceitful face of hope and of despair', in the words of *Ash-Wednesday* (III), for in *The Waste Land* each deceitfully signals the presence of the other. Shelter and relief are denied by the hypnotically sinister-seductive sound in the repetition of 'this red rock' and in the repetition and reversal between 'shadow under' and 'under the shadow'. 'Come in under the shadow' sounds welcoming ('come in') and at the same time threatening ('come under'). And there is a hint of threat in the slight auditory quickening as 'shadow' shrinks apprehensively to 'show' in 'I will show you'. This prophet ends up speaking in a pernickety syntax: there is something unsettling, fearsome even, in the disparity between the syntactic deliberation of these lines and their 'rising' panic:

> . . . I will show you something different from either
> Your shadow at morning striding behind you
> Or your shadow at evening rising to meet you;
> I will show you fear in a handful of dust.

These lines ally fearlessness ('striding'), even a sense of welcome ('rising to meet'), with fearfulness, intrepidity with trepidation. 'Striding' and 'rising to meet' convey different emotions depending on whether they are regarded as actions performed by the shadow or as actions performed by the thrower of the shadow. The emotion of fear is precisely articulated even in the effort to control it; indeed, the control expresses the fear.

The episode of the hyacinth garden (lines 35–42) is the nearest *The Waste Land* gets to *la poésie pure*. Most critics find it central to their reaction to the poem, but there are very different views as to what it portends. Framed by quotations from Wagner's *Tristan und Isolde*, it seems to conjure up a love experience: in the words of Grover Smith, 'The desolation in [the] second quotation . . . contrasts with the fresh breeze, a portent of happy love, in the first.'[16] But we should be wary of concluding from this that a Wagnerian mythic quest informs *The Waste Land*. Many critics see the episode as a visionary, timeless moment at the heart of a time-ridden poem; but it is an index of the episode's ambiguity that others, notably Kenner, hear in it a guilty, even sinister, register.[17] Michael Edwards rightly hears it both ways, and implies that its double nature is characteristic of the whole poem. This 'moment', he writes,

> seems to escape the toils of language, by looking to a possibility beyond speech. . . . 'Silence' at the end of its line rhymes

> semantically with the negatives at the end of the three previous lines. And 'I knew nothing' is not the same as 'I did not know anything': like silence, 'nothing' is positive, as in Mallarmé (or Lewis Carroll). A silence beyond words and a nothing beyond matter are attained in an apparently ecstatic vision of 'the heart of light' . . . .
>
> Yet, as many have suggested, the feeling moving through the . . . passage is itself troubled, ambiguous; even before the next line, *'Oed' und leer das Meer'*, negates it.
>
> It turns out to be implicated as much as any other [passage of the poem] in the fundamental ambiguity.[18]

It is consonant with this fundamental ambiguity that Conrad's title 'Heart of Darkness' does not simply act as a negative allusion behind Eliot's 'the heart of light': Conrad's words *shadow* Eliot's, like the morning or evening shadow that is both a part of and apart from you. Ambiguous too is the relationship between the hyacinth girl's words and what follows. '– Yet' (in '– Yet when we came back, late, from the hyacinth garden') seems to promise that the words just uttered by the hyacinth girl are about to be contradicted; but what follows contains nothing to indicate either that he did not give her hyacinths, or why 'they' should not call her 'the hyacinth girl'. If her words are stressed '*They* called me the hyacinth girl', the gist of what follows could be: 'but *I* would call you something more intimately intense, less like a sobriquet.' Or the contrast in 'yet' is between her ability to speak of the experience in the garden and his inability to speak.

How his silence is interpreted partly depends on how her words are heard. 'You gave me hyacinths first a year ago' approaches iambic pentameter; 'They called me the hyacinth girl' retreats from it. The latter is one of Eliot's characteristically unscannable and poker-faced lines. Depending on where you put the stress, it can sound strong in its remembering ('They called me the *hyacinth* girl'), or wistful ('They *called* me the hyacinth girl'). Or it can be emptied of all emphasis, toneless, flat, the 'hyacinths' of her first line sounding emphatic and bright, only to wither to a fading echo in her second as she makes her empty claim on him. Heard like that, she comes across as no Ophelia, but a hollow woman, a caricature of the romantic heroine.[19] As a response to a moment of remembered ecstasy the 'yet' introduces lines that even as they unfold acknowledge the agonising insufficiency of memory to re-animate and relive it; as a response to her wistfulness the 'yet' wants to gainsay the speaker's doubts and find validity in his memory of the girl. Memory and desire mix in the inscrutability of his words. Is he guilty of a lack of responsiveness to the hyacinth girl, or is he overwhelmed by a hyper-responsiveness? 'I could not / Speak': the line-break both strangles and releases the word 'Speak', both inhibits and frees utterance. 'Speak' struggles into speech. The words voice both the stricture of the phrase 'I could not' and the stricture overcome in the phrase 'I could not speak'. What happens to his eyes is 'fundamentally ambiguous'. 'My eyes failed': he was blinded with light; blindness can be positive, like 'nothing'. The source of sight blinds at the moment of insight. But 'my eyes *failed*': this way of putting it casts doubt on the moment of visionary insight even as it is being related. The equivalent moment in 'Burnt Norton' is truly visionary: 'The surface glittered out of heart of light', where 'out of' is enough out of the ordinary to intimate transcendence momentarily apprehended. 'I was neither / Living nor dead' intimates in-betweenness as much as transcendence, the word 'neither' hesitating at the end of a line, dwelling briefly on the state of neitherness.

But however ambiguous the memory of the hyacinth garden, the burden of the poetry is that the episode is bewilderingly irretrievable. However strong the desire, the moment cannot be relived, and therefore there is no point to the desiring. The start of 'Burnt Norton' would move beyond this position: 'What might have been and what has been / Point to one end, which is always present' – so much so that desire enlivens what did not happen: 'Footfalls echo in the memory / Down the passage which we did not take'.

Madame Sosostris gives a decisively different inflexion to the language of oracles and prophecy. But to call her a charlatan, even with support from the fact that her name is derived from the sham 'Sesostris' in Aldous Huxley's *Crome Yellow*, does not get her poetic measure.[20] Hers is the intimacy not of silence, but of talk. 'I could not / Speak' is not one of her problems. It is possible to imagine her appearing in the scenario depicted by Eliot about twenty years later, in 'The Dry Salvages' (V): 'To communicate with Mars, converse with spirits', 'Describe the horoscope, haruspicate or scry', 'release omens / By sortilege, or tea leaves, riddle the inevitable / With playing cards'. Some of these are features of *The Waste Land* too, but there the attitude towards them is not Elder Statesmanly as in 'The Dry Salvages', whatever else it is. Madame Sosostris is introduced with a finely tuned inscrutability:

> Madame Sosostris, famous clairvoyante,
> Had a bad cold, nevertheless
> Is known to be the wisest woman in Europe,
> With a wicked pack of cards.

'Nevertheless'! The *non sequitur* is scrupulously articulated: the poise of this weightily inconsequential conjunction between caesura and line-ending pays sly homage to Madame Sosostris's inconsequential powers. We wonder, too, how much weight to give to the phrase 'is known to be'. In *The Waste Land* much comes to us through hearsay: 'They *called* me the hyacinth girl', but . . . ; 'Is *known* to be the wisest woman', but. . . . The word 'wicked' captures a tone that might be used by such a one as 'Mrs. Equitone'. As Ricks observes, it is no coincidence that Madame Sosostris should be acquainted with someone with such a name.[21]

It is impishly 'wicked' of the poet to voice what purports to be the key to the whole poem through the intonationally inscrutable medium of Madame Sosostris, and with the clichéd device of a pack of cards. Eliot's note flags the device deviously:

> I am not familiar with the exact constitution of the Tarot pack of cards, from which I have obviously departed to suit my own

> convenience. The Hanged Man, a member of the traditional pack, fits my purpose in two ways: because he is associated in my mind with the Hanged God of Frazer, and because I associate him with the hooded figure in the passage of the disciples to Emmaus in Part V. The Phoenician Sailor and the Merchant appear later; also the 'crowds of people', and Death by Water is executed in Part IV. The Man with Three Staves (an authentic member of the Tarot pack) I associate, quite arbitrarily, with the Fisher King himself.

The manner of this note guards against the sort of decoding it indulges in. To be told at the outset that the poet is 'not familiar' with the code he claims to be employing does not inspire confidence. How one can 'obviously depart' from something 'the exact constitution' of which one is not familiar with is unclear. 'The Hanged Man ... fits my purpose' sounds capricious. 'Quite arbitrarily' gives the game away.

For all her talkativeness Madame Sosostris seems not to tell all. Her arch voice – and the inversion 'said she' colludes in the archness – has the intimacy of the button-holing sort, the nod and the wink. What status to give the clues in her vocal performance is impossible to determine:

> and this card,
> Which is blank, is something he carries on his back,
> Which I am forbidden to see. I do not find
> The Hanged Man.

These lines negate what they intimate. 'The Hanged Man' may correspond to sacrificial victim in a reading of *The Waste Land* as fertility ritual, but he gets into the poem only through Madame Sosostris's negative formulation 'I do not find'. Even so, Eliot's way with enjambment has its characteristically tricky say. 'I do not find the Hanged Man' does not have the same effect as Eliot's lineation, which is to make the Hanged Man sinisterly present even as he is being absented across the line-break.

Here, said she,
Is your card, the drowned Phoenician Sailor,
(Those are pearls that were his eyes. Look!)

John Lennard writes:

> the quotation from Ariel's song anticipates the redemptive sea-change that Phlebas will undergo. The parenthesis ... includes an imperative verb, and yet in context is elegiac and critical, exposing by contrast the summary professional patter from which it is syntactically and typographically separated. The more numinous Shakespearian diction diminishes the charlatanry of Madame Sosostris.... [The] parenthesis impugns and complicates the character of its speaker.[22]

That is one way of hearing the parenthesis. Another is to wonder if there is something off-key about appending the exclamation 'Look!' to Shakespeare's line about an eyeless corpse. Perhaps it is not Ariel's voice that is infecting Madame Sosostris's, but vice versa: it may be that what was numinous has been ironically gothicised. As a clairvoyante Madame Sosostris is appropriately concerned with eyes and with seeing, but clear-sightedness is not her forte: she picks out 'the one-eyed merchant' and she is 'forbidden to see'. She does 'see crowds of people', but one wonders whether their 'walking round in a ring' is not a crystal-gazing cliché. The rhythmless sound of 'I see crowds of people, walking round in a ring' is typical of the way her words frequently leave us wondering how to receive them. Her last line, 'One must be so careful these days', rivals 'They called me the hyacinth girl' in its unscannable flatness, and elicits this discerning description from Ricks: 'The rhythmical vacuum of the last line, its collusive sucking of us into a paralysing consciousness of any number of possible emphases, inflections or nuances ... in its refusal to come clean rhythmically, shows you fear in a hand of cards.'[23]

Madame Sosostris's voice has personality but equivocates; in contrast, the voice that proclaims 'Unreal City' sounds impersonal but is unequivocally sonorous. Partly the 'City' is 'Unreal' because the syntax which articulates it refuses, phantasmagorically, to stay fixed, so that the centre of gravity shifts from one line to the next as we read. Kenner pinpoints one of the effects: 'The unobtrusive "I" neither dominates nor creates this scene, being itself subordinated to a barely grammatical subordination.'[24] This effect is the result of some creatively critical honing, for originally the "I" did obtrude, precisely to dominate and create the scene. Originally the syntax was more stable:

> Unreal City, I have sometimes seen and see
> Under the brown fog of your winter dawn
> A crowd flow over London Bridge, so many,
> I had not thought death had undone so many.[25]

The repetition with variation in the filled-out first line makes the point, with deliberation, that how I see something now cannot be separated from how I have seen it in the past, that what I bring to it is part of my experience of it, that perception is affected by memory, that there is such a thing as the eye's mind as well as the mind's eye – deliberations which had preoccupied Eliot in his thesis on F. H. Bradley. (The same formula, 'Unreal City, I have seen and see', was also used for the City in 'The Fire Sermon'.)[26] Originally the cityscape was located in an experiencing, if unspecified, consciousness, so that external and internal worlds merged, cityscape blurring into mindscape. The first three lines about the City originally proceeded with syntactic efficiency as an invocation to the 'Unreal City', which, in oracularly quaint fashion, used the vocative case ('your winter dawn'), with 'I' as the subject, 'seen and see' as the verb, and the 'crowd', which flows over the bridge, as the object. Pound, whose marginal comments elsewhere in the drafts include such minor eruptions as 'Perhaps be *damned*' and 'make up yr. mind / you Tiresias if you know know damn well or else you dont', had a sharp ear for dithering, and questioned the whole line 'Unreal City, I have sometimes seen and see'. His pragmatic doubts inspired one of the boldest, and in its turn pragmatically brilliant, poetic strokes of *The Waste Land*. The honing of these lines testifies to Eliot's instinctive feel for the accurately unusual, to his ability to deviate from the ordinary just enough to reveal an extraordinary sensibility. Pound may have thought that he was pushing Eliot in the direction of clarity, and so he was, in a way, but not towards clarity of statement. Removing the dithering phrase 'I have sometimes seen and see' transforms the dither into a more radical apprehension of 'unreality'. Now the syntax, disturbed by the removal of that phrase, enacts a disturbed and disturbing apprehension with compelling stealth. The straightforward has been ever so slightly dislocated, with hauntingly disorienting effect. In the published text the forthright address to the 'Unreal City' seems to offer the promise of syntactic closure which, as we read on, goes unsettlingly ungratified. The words turn out, after all, not to be an invocation. They float free, suspended in unreality, not quite a vocative any longer, syntactically not quite connected, a grammatical equivalent of 'unreality', of the hallucinatory scenes that are to follow. And whereas originally 'the brown fog' had been grammatically subordinated to the seeing 'I' and the flowing crowd, now, in its grammatically more indefinite and less dependent form, suspended between commas, it becomes a presence in its own right, not possessed by the City (not '*your* winter dawn'), but in possession of it, overpowering and overshadowing it (the City being, for a moment, grammatically 'under' the fog).

The dissolving of sure grammatical articulation in the published text means that nothing is subordinated to anything else: City, fog, crowd, each looms up in turn as the focus of attention, in syntactic and phantasmagoric disconnection. The central perspective in 'I have sometimes seen and see' has disappeared, so that City, fog and crowd take on a life of their own. In particular, the 'I' no longer sees 'a crowd flow'; instead, 'A crowd flowed', independent of any experiencing consciousness and only in loose syntactic connection with the fog of the previous line. A consciousness now declares itself only in the fourth line of the paragraph; but, after the voice out of the void of the first three lines, the personal testimony of 'I had not thought death had undone so many' is disturbing. This line (a version of *Inferno* III, 55–7), syntactically an afterthought, turns into the weighty central thought, a new centre of gravity which magnetises the previous lines towards itself. 'A winter dawn' ushers in, not another day, but, with ghostly onomatopoeia ('un*d*er', '*d*awn', '*d*eath', 'un*d*one'), the thought of death. The repetition of 'so many' at the end of two consecutive lines signifies a deeply pondering consciousness. The first 'so many' sounds awestruck and incredulous, the second stoically confirmatory. The closure is so absolute as to discomfort with its finality, 'a dead sound on the final stroke' indeed. As death becomes the centre of gravity, an unlively syntax gets impressively to work. The members of the crowd do not actively die; they are passive before death, which has 'undone' them with a baldly undemonstrative verb (a straight translation of Dante's 'disfatta'). Then, with the dead hand of the passive construction in 'Sighs, short and infrequent, were exhaled', the crowd does not do the sighing but is the passive medium for sighs. Impersonal death then proceeds ineluctably with another syntactically stealthy wrench: the subject-less verb 'Flowed' begins a new sentence, resuming the 'flowed' of two sentences earlier ('A crowd flowed'). 'Flowed' sounds effortless: this is the journey of so many. But the repetition has a contrary effect, the second 'flowed' having the feel of starting up again, enacting the effortful progress of this crowd of non-pilgrims. In between the first 'flowed' and the second have intervened the thought of death and the rhythmically trudging iambics of 'And each man fixed his eyes before his feet', a line that sounds as if it is treading 'the pavement in a dead patrol' (in the words of that other hallucinatory Dantean and otherworldly vision of London pedestrians, in 'Little Gidding'). The second 'flowed' inaugurates lines of poetry that do not flow, but reinforce the wearisome tread of 'And each man fixed his eyes before his feet':

> Flowed up the hill and down King William Street,
> To where Saint Mary Woolnoth kept the hours
> With a dead sound on the final stroke of nine.

Between 'Unreal City' and 'stroke of nine' the rhythmic progression is from an uncertain but impressive approximation of iambics – how, for instance, do you scan 'Under the brown fog of a winter dawn'? – to a doom-laden iambic certainty.

The ensuing lines about the corpse (69–76) do not, however, sound dead, even if they speak of the dead. Analysis might point out the formal tidying up going on in these lines, the fact that the end of 'The Burial of the Dead' knows its beginning: the sprouting dead recalls the dead land breeding lilacs; in both beginning and end there is the disturbance of spring; and in both, digging up the past, the dead, is resisted even as it is contemplated (the quotation from *The White Devil* intimating that it is cruel to dig it up again, as April is cruel to stir dull roots). But the last lines of 'The Burial of the Dead' ward off this sort of analysis even as they gesture at it, by their springy rhythm which gives them a frenetic, unhinged air, by their sinister talk of sprouting corpses, by their speaking of the dead with a macabre sort of life, by the fact that they are spoken to someone possibly named after a hat, 'Stetson'. Unnervingly, this spoof version of a fertility ritualist turns out to be, or turns into, the reader – or the reader as conceived of by Baudelaire in the last line of his poem 'Au Lecteur'. 'The Burial of the Dead' signs off with a foreign flourish that holds us at a distance as much as it draws us in. If the poetry purports to find us out by quoting the line from Baudelaire, it does so in self-mockery. Baudelaire's poem ends by declaring our ugliest and most wicked vice thus:

> C'est l'Ennui! – l'oeil chargé d'un pleur involontaire,
> Il rêve d'échafauds en fumant son houka.
> Tu le connais, lecteur, ce monstre délicat,
> – Hypocrite lecteur, – mon semblable, mon frère!

(it is Boredom, *Tedium vitae*, who with an unwilling tear in his eye dreams of gibbets as he smokes his pipe. You know him, Reader, you know that fastidious monster – O hypocritical Reader, my fellow-man and brother!)[27]

Is it *ennui* that has been responsible for the ghoulish imaginings we have just been witnessing in 'The Burial of the Dead'? *The Waste Land* often sounds as though it is mocking its own creations, for instance, and especially its sprouting corpse and the whole matter of what Eliot's poker-faced note calls 'vegetation ceremonies' to which 'certain references' are made. The poem intimates that at some level it suspects it is demonstrating what it denigrates, that it is itself an exemplar of hyper self-consciousness, a true product of 'the present self-conscious century'.[28] In as much as we get our thrills out of reading *The Waste Land* we are party to this process: 'Hypocrite lecteur'.

Behind the allusion to Baudelaire is a matter that was to become the motivation for much of Eliot's thinking on religion and society. In his essay on Baudelaire (1930) he was to find in ennui a religious dimension:

> His *ennui* may of course be explained, as everything can be explained in psychological or pathological terms; but it is also, from the opposite point of view, a true form of *acedia*, arising from the unsuccessful struggle towards the spiritual life.[29]

At the time of *The Waste Land*'s composition Eliot would no doubt have thought of it in psychological or pathological terms; many later readers – with the probable inclusion of the poet himself in retrospect – have read it 'from the opposite point of view' in terms of a 'struggle', successful or not, 'towards the spiritual life'.

II

'A Game of Chess'

The blatant literariness of the opening paragraph of 'A Game of Chess' would draw us in, turning us into hypocritical readers in connivance with the knowing poet. *The Waste Land* has become so familiar that we forget how breathtakingly impertinent, and risky, it is to mimic one of the most famous speeches in Shakespeare's work. Enobarbus says that the sight of Cleopatra on her barge 'beggared all description', and Eliot's impertinence of allusion beggars belief.[1] But if the paragraph begins by sounding like a set piece soliciting applause, it soon turns into something other, mocking its parodic formula. It rises above its literary occasion with lines that are 'fattened' with what begins to sound like the exaggeratedly 'poetical'. The reader might be tempted to respond 'A periphrastic study in a worn-out poetical fashion', as Eliot was famously to do of a paragraph in 'East Coker', except that here, in 'A Game of Chess', periphrasis and the outmoded 'way of putting it' lead to the charge, not of 'not very satisfactory', but of a superabundance, a glut, of satisfaction. Claustrophobic syntax and diction conjure up 'the room enclosed'. The writing indeed beggars the act of description, making the pictorial serve other ends. The more the visual detail accumulates, the less we can be sure of what we are seeing. Our 'senses' become 'troubled, confused / And drowned', in keeping with the poetry's confusions of linguistic and grammatical 'sense'. Words describing the scenic props equally well describe the style, which comes over as 'synthetic', 'burnished' and highly 'wrought', 'glittering' with 'antique', rare and artificial-sounding words such as 'fruited', 'Cupidon' (which the OED defines as 'A "beau" or "Adonis"', giving as its only example Byron's *Don Juan*, XV, xii), 'candelabra', 'unguent' (which here seems to be used as an adjective, meaning 'in ointment form', although the OED records only one such usage, in its Supplement, and that in 1931 by Hilaire Belloc), 'laquearia' (from the *Aeneid* I, as Eliot's note points out), 'coffered' (which, in the sense of 'furnished with sunk panels', the OED defines as archaic), 'carvèd', 'sylvan' (from *Paradise Lost*, as another note remarks).

The 'candle-flames' are 'prolonged', and so are the syntactic periods of this opening paragraph. The first sentence lasts nine lines, but the main verb ('glowed') comes early on, in the second line, and the subordinate clause beginning 'where the glass' prolongs itself towards its continually suspended verb 'doubled' in the sixth line, with three other clauses, one for each line, intervening, one of them enclosed in parentheses. Then, just as we feel we are reaching closure, the sentence picks up again with 'reflecting light', and yet again with 'as / The glitter ... rose', the clauses doubling and reflecting back on themselves:

> Reflecting light upon the table as
> The glitter of her jewels rose to meet it

Here the second line rises to meet the first with the word 'it'. This sounds like the end of the sentence, but it is not, and for one last time it takes a breath and continues for another line, the words 'rich profusion' characterising the whole of the sentence they are concluding.

In the next lines (86–93) the syntax is even more claustrophobic, enclosing the reader in a troubling and confusing doubleness. The woman's seductive wiles come across not only in linguistic innuendo that 'peeps out' at us (as the 'Cupidon peeped out'), in such words as 'unstoppered', 'lurked', 'unguent', 'liquid', 'fattening', 'stirring', but also in troublingly wily confusions of syntax that trap and enclose. The glut of words ending in '-ed' is one cause of the confusion:

> In vials of ivory and coloured glass
> Unstoppered, lurked her strange synthetic perfumes,
> Unguent, powdered, or liquid – troubled, confused
> And drowned the sense in odours; stirred by the air

The word 'glass' is sandwiched between the adjectival past participles 'coloured' and 'unstoppered', the latter sounding like a 'poetic' inversion across the line-break. Then comes 'lurked', which, following straight on from another '-ed' word, fleetingly stirs up a grammatical confusion before settling down, not as another adjectival participle, but as the sentence's main verb in the past indicative. 'Powdered' re-establishes an adjectival feel; and then come those two '-ed' words, 'troubled, confused', which are truly confusing. Since they follow an indeterminate dash, how they attach themselves grammatically to the rest of the sentence is uncertain. At first they sound as though they may be adjectival participles like 'unstoppered' and 'powdered'; but when we read on over the line-break they turn into past indicatives like 'drowned' (in 'And drowned the sense in odours') and like 'lurked' in the previous line.[2] At the same time the dash has freed the words 'troubled, confused' from strict syntactical articulation, allowing them to conjure up the emotional state of one whose senses are about to be seductively 'drowned'. Again, the sentence prolongs itself hypnotically: the word 'stirred', coming immediately after a semi-colon, is in syntactic limbo until anchored by the words 'these ascended' at the end of the next line, although even then we have to double back four lines to identify 'these' as the 'perfumes', still working their grammatical confusions. They give rise to a 'strange synthetic' grammar. For all the activity of the verbs hereabouts ('flung', for instance, is inappropriately vigorous for what is being flung), there is little sense of articulate movement. The plethora of verbs and adjectival participles – 'stirred', 'freshened', 'ascended', 'fattening', 'prolonged', 'flung', 'stirring', 'coffered' – does not freshen or stir.

On the contrary it stultifies. Symptomatically, the perfumes begin by being 'stirred' and end by 'stirring' in the same sentence four lines later.

This is a decadent and stifling syntax to convey a decadent and stifling sexuality. The confusing verbal and visual properties continue into the next lines: the burning 'sea-wood' gets swimmingly associated with the 'carvèd dolphin' two lines later, and the word 'framed' (in 'framed by the coloured stone', line 95) hintingly predicts the pictorial representation of 'the change of Philomel' that is to follow. But the hypnotic rhetoric and the satirically literary strain stir and trouble a more compassionate emotion: with beautifully undemonstrative economy, 'sad light' registers not only that the light is low, but that the emotions are too. Up to this point the pastiche antique has tended to camouflage and deaden what is 'going on': the reader has been put under stylistic hypnosis, anaesthetised to the forces at play by an aureate rhetoric of yesteryear. 'Above the antique mantel was displayed' is a way of putting it that hides with coy literariness what it would display; so does the next line with its 'gave upon' and 'sylvan', even if we pay attention to Eliot's note alerting us to the Miltonic allusion and feel behind the words 'sylvan scene' the presence of Satan when he first reached Eden, intent on humankind's fall. 'The change of Philomel' is an expression that shields a violent reality behind the literary mask of the Ovidian 'tale' of metamorphosis. Even the explicitness of 'by the barbarous king / So rudely forced' is equivocal, 'rudely' being in danger of diminishing the barbarity of the sexual violence to unmannerly impoliteness, the word 'so', if given a conversational inflexion, denoting scorn rather than repulsion, a lesser, rather than a greater, censoriousness.

Then, cutting through all the hypnotic artifice and syntactic confusion come the startlingly clear, syntactically direct words 'yet there the nightingale / Filled all the desert with inviolable voice'. As John Lennard has pointed out, Eliot's speaking picture of Philomel probably owes something to *Purgatorio* X, where a series of friezes, including that of Philomel, are 'enabled by God to narrate the stories they depict'. Thus her story is made to speak out of the past to us now, bringing 'the tragic and criminal past into the empty and guilty present'.[3] The story still cries out with 'inviolable voice', testing our reactions. The violated Philomel, tongue cut off, unable to put her story into words, nevertheless expresses her grief in inviolable song; and the contrast between the inviolable simplicity of these words and the stylistic and syntactic violations, the elaborate profusion and confusion, of the writing up to this point in 'A Game of Chess', is an act of poetic empathy. *La poésie pure* takes on a moral and sexual strain. Wordy elaboration gives way to verbal simplicity and even, in the sounds 'Jug Jug', to some sort of approximation of wordlessness, the nightingale's song without words. The contrast signifies the opposites between and within which *The Waste Land* exists, between its hubbub of voices and the speechlessness, 'the silence', of 'I could not / Speak'. If 'the desert' is in a sense the poem itself, 'stony rubbish' composed of 'a heap of broken images', then to fill 'all the desert with inviolable voice' represents the poet's uttermost wish.

But inviolability of voice is in the ear of the listener. 'Jug Jug' can sound like sound without meaning, nonsense syllables; or 'in Elizabethan poetry' it can be, in Southam's words, 'a way of representing bird-song', or, alternatively, 'a crude joking reference to sexual intercourse'.[4] But we have been reading, not Elizabethan poetry, but something like it, a pastiche; and we wonder how to hear or to take the words 'Jug Jug', whether we, or the poetry, or both, are not being made fun of (an experience not unique to this part of *The Waste Land*, to be sure). But just this uncertainty is at the heart of the poetry hereabouts. The change from the hypnotic lushness of sounding iambics and archaic diction to a more direct utterance is accompanied by a disturbed and disturbing move from past to present, so that what had seemed like an orotund literary evocation catches us off guard. This move happens with breathtakingly deft and underspoken ellipsis, and we barely realise what is taking place until after the event: 'And still she cried, and still the world pursues, / "Jug Jug" to dirty ears.' The underspeaking happens in what at first sounds like the emphatic repetition of 'still'. But the two 'stills' mirror and reverse each other in astonishing bewilderment. Although after her transformation Philomel's voice was inviolable, although she could not be violated further, even so (the first 'still') she went on crying grievously; and yet (the second 'still'), in spite of the grievous story of Philomel, the world continues even now (the second 'still' having this sense as well) to pursue her. '"Jug Jug" to dirty ears' conflates the pure notation of birdsong and the prurient notation of sexual slang. Philomel's cry does not sound grievous to those who want to hear differently. The innocence of 'cried' cries out even as it continues to be violated, to be transformed in the ears of the 'dirty' world in pursuit. The nature of that voice depends on the disposition of the hearer – as the nature of the whole of *The Waste Land* is in the ear of the 'Hypocrite lecteur'. The sly interweaving of past and present, the deft move from 'cried' to 'pursues', signals how the mythic past still lives, unresolved, in the unmythic present, even as we try to resolve the finally unresolvable syntax.

It is with another deft stroke that Eliot uses the Dantean speaking picture: 'And other withered stumps of time / Were told upon the walls'. With shocking and cruel brevity 'withered stumps' punningly conjures up Philomel's tongue-stump. The fact that these wordless stumps are 'told' redoubles the irony, savagely. For all their muteness they speak to later ages, enabling their stories to be 'told', telling of the untellable, speaking of the unspeakable; and they act as an example to the poet of how to utter the unutterable, how to endure and overcome the sense of 'I could not / Speak'. Conversely, the pictures can conjure silence in Gothically mysterious posture: 'staring forms / Leaned out, leaning, hushing the room enclosed.' This syntax strains with importunity. The repetitive phrase 'Leaned out, leaning' leans beggingly towards us; 'leaning' is grammatically and emotionally in suspension. The sentence is frustrated even as it implores. To appreciate the economy with which the strained and straining emotions are conveyed here, it helps to read Eliot's earlier thoughts:

> And other tales, from the old stumps and bloody ends of time
> Were told upon the walls, where staring forms
> Leaned out, and hushed the room and closed it in.[5]

'[S]tumps and bloody ends of time' does not have the underspoken horror of 'stumps of time'; 'hushing' instead of 'hushed' keeps the hush and its expectantly tense emotions in play; 'the room enclosed' has an air of engulfing claustrophobia missing from the sound of closing finality in 'closed it in'. And the early version does not linger importunately and eerily, as the final text does, on the action of leaning.

If the syntax at the start of this paragraph is confused so as to drown the senses, at its end it is confused so as to prepare for a very definite sense, the accusing line 'Glowed into words, then would be savagely still':

> Under the firelight, under the brush, her hair
> Spread out in fiery points
> Glowed into words, then would be savagely still.

Confusingly, the parallel between the two 'under's is grammatical and verbal only. 'Spread' at first comes across as the main verb, then seems to recede into a past participle with the appearance of the verb 'Glowed' at the start of the next line, but then retrieves something of its first status with the final clause beginning 'then' (as if to say, 'her hair spread out, then glowed, then would be . . .'). The effect is shifting and unstill until that final line. Originally the second line quoted read 'Spread out in little fiery points of will', and the deletion of the words 'of will' (a response to Pound's comment 'dogmatic deduction but wobbly as well') alerts us to the fact that there is plenty of wilfulness in these lines without it needing to be spelt out.[6]

Glowing into words reverses what was going on earlier in 'A Game of Chess', where the pictures of Philomel and of others unspecified ('And other withered stumps') 'tell' stories for our edification; in the lines just quoted the reverse happens and the woman's 'words' are made visible in their glowing. And her speech does glow with a savage stillness:

> 'My nerves are bad to-night. Yes, bad. Stay with me.
> 'Speak to me. Why do you never speak. Speak.
> 'What are you thinking of? What thinking? What?
> 'I never know what you are thinking. Think.'

Michael Edwards comments:

> We may take this non-realistic passage as the mimesis nevertheless of a psychological state and a conversational gambit. But we ought also to notice that it is a piece of language that fades. Each of the last three lines peters out in a diminished echo of itself.[7]

There is certainly diminishment in the notation of these lines, although are they not more glowingly savage than 'fades' allows? Each of the last three lines quoted is fined down to a sharp monosyllable and an accusing silence. This is a different silence from 'the heart of light, the silence' which transfused the episode of the hyacinth girl, just as the nothing that fills the head of the silent listener to the woman's neurotic utterances, his inner vacancy, his inward and unspoken 'Nothing again nothing', is different from the nothing of 'I knew nothing', the no thing that is known in the hyacinth garden. The woman is hypersensitively attuned in her echoing of the man's vacant thoughts, with her 'Do / You know nothing? Do you see nothing? Do you remember / Nothing?' The episode, not a monologue, but not a dialogue either though an exchange of sorts, is both 'non-realistic' and hyper-realistic, a formal notation of communicative and emotional stale-mate. The woman's speech takes on an unnaturalistic rhythm, anticipating Eliot's experiments with rhythmical dialogue in *Sweeney Agonistes*. The episode also reads like a recollection of the one-sided 'dialogue' of 'Portrait of a Lady', in which the woman's words are accompanied by the introspective 'dull tom-tom' in the man's brain, 'Absurdly hammering a prelude of its own'. The tom-tom of this episode in 'A Game of Chess' insists on recalling, among other things, the line from *The Tempest* that was teasingly quoted by Madame Sosostris, 'Those are pearls that were his eyes.' The woman's mute listener may be in a psychological Hades ('I think we are in rats' alley / Where the dead men lost their bones'), but he also becomes warily aware of the figure he is cutting. Even as the poetry 'remembers' Ariel's line, it becomes conscious that that is what it is doing: 'O O O O that Shakespeherian Rag – / It's so elegant / So intelligent'. A countervailing level of discourse breaks in here with its ironic perspective. As so often happens in *The Waste Land*, the poetry turns on itself, aware that it is going through its poetic paces.

The pub scene comes across as vocal performance. Only a foreigner recently settled in England could have heard the barman's words, 'HURRY UP PLEASE ITS TIME', with enough freshness to be able to make poetry out of them – a new poetry for the sense of an ending. Paradoxically this, one of the most mimetically 'realistic' episodes in *The Waste Land*, is also one of the most self-conscious. The episode is symptomatic of a poem that is 'in different voices', whose essential quality is its vocalness: the word 'said' occurs, in gossipy fashion, fifteen times. 'HURRY UP PLEASE ITS TIME' wittily becomes the voice to end all voices. The barman's words break into and break up the narrative, their capitalization typographically indicating their sonorous and possibly portentous register. They contribute meanings to the narrative unintended by its narrator, a procedure assisted by the lack of quotation marks around the reported speech. At first they break in grammatically, merging with the bar-side monologue and reinforcing the sense of time running out before Albert's return; then they add depth to the intimations of mortality, the fear of turning 'antique' and losing your man; then, re-entering after the intimations of abortion, they add a quasi-apocalyptic note to the line 'What you get married for if you don't want children?', a note which intensifies as the bar closes. Finally, the demotic 'Goonight' shades into the Shakespearian 'Good night, ladies, good night, sweet ladies, good night, good night', and the poetry withdraws from the present to invoke one of those stumps of time,

Ophelia's madness and suicidal death by drowning. Social satire moves towards sympathy, and 'Shakespeherian Rag' modulates into a graver music. Ophelia's lingering farewell, by addressing the denizens of the pub as 'sweet ladies', both gives them dignity and heightens the pathetic irony of their lives. As has been frequently observed, *The Waste Land* does not simply weigh a degenerate present against a pristine past; rather, the past haunts the present, and the way in which Ophelia's words hauntingly emerge out of and merge into the mêlée of voices that makes up 'A Game of Chess' is symptomatic. With that final line the poetry takes on the intonation of one who, inviolably, made music out of her suffering: 'And still she cried.'[8] And still *The Waste Land* cries as it ventriloquises a broken music from those who suffer.

III

'The Fire Sermon'

'The Fire Sermon' foregrounds its writerly frustrations and pretensions. The first verse-paragraph sounds as though it is trying on various poetic styles, in so doing giving voice to the mixed emotions of irony and pathos. In Spenser's full-throated 'Prothalamion' there can be no distance between the 'I' of 'Sweet Themmes run softlie, till I end my Song' and the singer of that song (unless in the sixth stanza, which consists of the 'lay' sung by one of the Thames Nymphs, although this song within a song is clearly signalled). But when Spenser's line finds its way into Eliot's poem the 'I' is set at liberty. In its new context the line, quoted twice, is uncertain not only as to speaker but also as to intonation. Spenser's poem has been ironised, many feel: his Nymphs do honour 'Against the Brydale day' in a harmonious pastoral vision, whereas the vision of 'The Fire Sermon' is a morbid one of sexual violation, inanition and disharmony; Eliot's nymphs have been compromised by the company and context they keep. Yet at its first occurrence, 'The nymphs are departed' (line 175) sounds genuinely plangent; only when it recurs four lines later, after the catalogue of river detritus, does its slightly stilted expression ('are departed', not 'have departed') more certainly take on an arch air. When Eliot first quotes the line by Spenser (at line 176) the plangent vies with the ironic. Indeed, in its new context Spenser's line possesses an extraordinary pathos not present in 'Prothalamion', where it has more the beautiful formality of a repeated refrain. But then towards the end of the first paragraph of 'The Fire Sermon' the poet begins to play around with Spenser's line, deflating it – but in so doing also deflating his own achievement: 'Sweet Thames, run softly till I end my song, / Sweet Thames, run softly, for I speak not loud or long' – lines which can only pull themselves together by moving into the ironic insouciance of Eliot's Marvellian rewrite, which, far from debunking the lines from 'To His Coy Mistress', attempts a contemporary equivalent for the comprehensiveness and penetration which Eliot found in them:[1] 'But at my back in a cold blast I hear / The rattle of the bones, and chuckle spread from ear to ear.'

Audible in the opening lines of 'The Fire Sermon' are other kinds of 'chuckle', less akin to the death-rattle. Is 'other testimony of summer nights' a neutral 'et cetera' to the river detritus listed in the preceding two lines as being absent, or is it a coy periphrasis? This sort of question is both invited and warded off. Most would probably agree with Southam that 'the rhetorical ring' of 'The river's tent is broken' suggests 'solemn overtones of meaning' that go beyond 'the immediate, visual image', perhaps, as he suggests, 'the loss ... of some sacred or mystic quality'; and he goes on to cite the Old Testament's use of 'tent' to mean tabernacle.[2] But perhaps the 'loss' is, less mystically, the human ritual which the Nymph's song in 'Prothalamion' calls 'loves couplement', a suggestion supported by the post-coital sound of the next words, 'the last fingers of leaf / Clutch and sink into the wet bank.' These opening lines combine the risqué and the resonant with unnerving sang-froid. 'By the waters of Leman I sat down and wept...' pulls out the lachrymose stop with questionable force, unless the trailing dots give us pause to recall that a leman is a mistress or prostitute. The whole of this verse-paragraph is an impressive vocal performance of emotional release and holding back, of flowing and retention, as the voice searches, moves into deeper registers, stalls, checks itself, lets itself go again, winsome, wry, upbraiding, plangent and caustic by turns. The miracle is that the verse can turn and turn about like this and still retain, triumphantly, a poetic coherence.

The high-sounding is in continual danger of collapsing. The creeping rat with its 'slimy belly', the 'White bodies naked on the low damp ground / And bones cast in a little low dry garret': the horror, conveyed as it is by such adjectival amplitude, has a Gothic air. To fish 'round behind the gashouse' sounds like 'poetic' straining for the 'unpoetic', especially if you are of royal blood. But then the royal strain is curiously elaborated: 'Musing upon the king my brother's wreck / And on the king my father's death before him.' The genealogical flurry has an air of raising questions inappropriate at this memorial moment. Do we not chuckle when, perhaps wondering why Eliot has expanded Shakespeare's line 'Weeping again the King my father's wreck' into two lines that kill off a royal brother also, we come across this kind of explanation? –

> In *The Tempest* it is the King, Alonso, who Ferdinand thinks has been drowned, so that a further identification makes the 'death' of Alonso the 'death' of Ferdinand as well. The quester is consequently in some sense about to re-enact his own father's misfortune. One may here detect the rudiments of a cyclical pattern.[3]

Yet the lines do tease the reader into this sort of thought, and most commentators on *The Waste Land* find themselves from time to time practising the higher sleuthing mode of criticism, often in spite of themselves. But it is more appropriate to listen to the poetry in the act of sounding out remembered, or half-remembered, cadences: like the oracle, the poet riddles as well as pronounces. The poetry frequently carries itself forward by the sound it makes. 'And bones cast in a little low dry garret, / Rattled by the rat's foot only, year to year': 'garret' sparks 'rattled' which sparks 'rat's foot'. When the second echo of 'To His Coy Mistress' comes in the next line (196), it sounds partly inspired by the rhyme with 'year' as well as by a sense of the different sort of coyness modern nymphs get up to, and by the evident irony of turning Marvell's tetrameter line 'But at my back I always hear' into a pentameter by deflating and extending 'always' into 'from time to time'; the effect is to reduce Marvell's 'Deserts of vast eternity' to this metropolitan waste land. The fullness of the rhyme, unexpected in a mostly unrhymed verse-paragraph, is suspect: the oracular courts the jingle, an effect augmented in the next two lines, about 'horns', 'motors', Sweeney and Mrs Porter, with their extension of the rhyming couplet, and the possibly phallic innuendo in 'horns'.

This poetry comes across as being aware of its composite nature, that this is a voice composed of other voices, unable to settle into a single register, shifting quixotically, scornful and lamenting by turns:

> O the moon shone bright on Mrs. Porter
> And on her daughter
> They wash their feet in soda water
> *Et O ces voix d'enfants, chantant dans la coupole!*

Ten lines later 'Mr. Eugenides, the Smyrna merchant', is reported as speaking 'in demotic French'; the line intoned here from Verlaine's sonnet 'Parsifal' is in distinctly undemotic French. Stefan Hawlin describes well how to hear this poetry. Noting the shift from the memory of an Australian ballad about Mrs Porter the brothel-keeper and her daughter the prostitute, to the line by Verlaine, he writes: 'It may have been the contrast of two rhythms, one syncopated and the other composed, that suggested the formulation of the lines, for a contrast of the rhythms is a part of the meaning'; and he goes on to argue that the sounds of the cars 'are transformed into "ces voix d'enfants, chantant dans la coupole" (the spiritual uplift experienced by Parsifal after his ascetic quest). The pathos of the irony is enacted by the musical contrast between a jingle and a truly sonorous line.'[4] Such contrasts testify to an uneasy attempt to focus an emotional response to the poem's sexual waste land. Just how sharp the contrast is here can be indicated by a bawdier version of the Australian ballad, which has been recorded, cautiously, thus:

> The moon shines bright on Mrs. Porter
> And on her daughter:
> She washes out her –––– in soda water,
> And so she oughta,
> To keep it clean.[5]

Such are the demotic voices that *The Waste Land* at once echoes and suppresses. As Southam explains,

> In the Grail Legend, the choir of children sings at the ceremony of the foot-washing which precedes the restoration of the wounded Anfortas (the Fisher King) by the Knight Parzifal and the lifting of the curse from the waste land.[6]

But Eliot's waste land is still cursed, and the line by Verlaine breaks in as a discordant, or, rather, inappropriately concordant, note between a very different foot-washing song, and syllables that, in their realm of non-sense, seem to sound, to plead for, registers beyond the demotic, where utterance is voided of human meaning and suffering: 'Twit twit twit / Jug jug . . .'. The nightingale's song of 'A Game of Chess' recurs in 'The Fire Sermon' (lines 203–6) as syllables out of nowhere, possibly as ironic undertone to those childish voices from Verlaine's poem. If the nightingale's monosyllables sound as if they are straining for the condition of pure sound, trying to escape the seedy sex of 'The Fire Sermon', they are pursued and held back by the idea of rape that attaches to 'Jug Jug' from 'A Game of Chess'. And even if the simple plaint of 'Tereu' approaches *la poésie pure*, it cannot escape the violation of explanation. Southam writes, '*Tereu* (the Latin vocative form of Tereus) refers to King Tereus, who raped . . . Philomela.'[7] Even the purest sounding of utterances is sullied by allusive depths.

Eliot's notorious note about Tiresias testifies to authorial anxiety; as advice on how to read *The Waste Land* it is misleading:

> Tiresias, although a mere spectator and not indeed a 'character', is yet the most important personage in the poem, uniting all the rest. Just as the one-eyed merchant, seller of currants, melts into the Phoenician Sailor, and the latter is not wholly distinct from

> Ferdinand Prince of Naples, so all the women are one woman, and the two sexes meet in Tiresias. What Tiresias *sees*, in fact, is the substance of the poem.

The difference between 'character' and 'personage' is made no clearer by the placing of inverted commas round the former word. Southam argues that this note 'draws our attention to the fluidity of the point-of-view of *The Waste Land*'.[8] But if this is so, it does so in spite of itself, for it reads as though it wants to do just the opposite, to draw attention away from that 'fluidity' by presenting Tiresias as the unifying consciousness, thus allaying not only the reader's sense of bewilderment at the poem's lack of a central perspective, but also, it seems, the author's when contemplating his creation.

But if the note is unconvincing in its attempt to assuage common expectations about unity, it nevertheless hints significantly at the epistemological assumptions behind this sort of poetry. 'What Tiresias *sees* . . . is the substance of the poem': the object of interest here is as much the state of mind of the perceiver as the state of the 'personages' perceived. In the drafts of 'The Fire Sermon', between the paragraph beginning 'Unreal City' about Mr Eugenides, and the paragraph containing Tiresias, there originally appeared a vatic apostrophe to London. It is a vulnerable example of the 'unreality' of *The Waste Land*'s urban vision, and no doubt Eliot excised it partly because it strikes the oracular note with a risible solemnity which does not, like many of the prophetic passages remaining in the final text, reveal any consciousness of its vulnerability. (Pound commented B--ll--S against the excised passage, which contains such lines as 'London, your people is bound upon the wheel!', and 'Phantasmal gnomes, burrowing in brick and stone and steel!') But the excised passage does revealingly state that London 'lives only in the awareness of the observing eye', which, even if lax as a line of poetry, testifies to Eliot's epistemological preoccupation, especially as he worried away at the passage before finally abandoning it, at one time trying out the variant 'transformations' for 'awareness': to be aware of something is to transform it.[9] Kenner, commenting on the excised passage, writes that it 'specifies in what respect the City is Unreal: unreal the way sensate accretions are unreal for Plato. . . . Its whole life has been levelled down to the plane of sensation.'[10] 'Unreal sensate accretions' is an apt gloss on the epistemology of the whole of *The Waste Land*, which gives the impression of existing primarily 'in the awareness of the observing eye'; an apt gloss also on Eliot's note quoting from Bradley: 'My external sensations are no less private to my self than are my thoughts or my feelings. In either case my experience falls within my own circle, a circle closed on the outside.'

This is particularly the effect of the episode of the typist and clerk. The object of interest becomes as much the state of mind of the observer as the participants in the scene who are being observed. Indeed, such subject–object distinctions are tenuous: the scene is a mindscape, a projection of the 'zone of consciousness',[11] in Kenner's phrase, which at this point in the poem is called 'Tiresias'. The 'awareness' entirely dominates the 'observing eye', which becomes inward-looking, and the result is an internalised 'vision'. Eliot has given a psychological twist to the myth of the physically blind man turned 'seer'. If his Tiresias sounds like prophet turned voyeur, the voyeurism – like all voyeurism – has a solipsistically onanistic trace.

> At the violet hour, when the eyes and back
> Turn upward from the desk, when the human engine waits
> Like a taxi throbbing waiting,
> I Tiresias, though blind, throbbing between two lives,
> Old man with wrinkled female breasts, can see
> At the violet hour, the evening hour that strives
> Homeward, and brings the sailor home from sea,
> The typist home at teatime, clears her breakfast, lights
> Her stove, and lays out food in tins.

These lines (215–23) impress with their boldly sly effects. 'Eyes and back' is a slightly disturbing collocation: the synecdoche sounds eerie in its depersonalising, calling uneasy attention to the organs of sight which, we are about to learn, in Tiresias's case are deficient. In the original layout, in quatrains, the 'rhyming' of 'see' and 'sea' sounded like a desperate remedy to a formal problem. But in the more sporadic rhyming of the final text, where there is no such formal expectation, the 'see/sea' homophone subliminally plays on the matter of seeing.[12] The line 'Like a taxi throbbing waiting' rhythmically both throbs and waits, reaching forward and holding back. The prose sense is 'when the human engine waits like a throbbing taxi', but Tiresias's way of putting it, the bold 'waits/waiting' repetition at the line-endings, intensifies the apprehensive waiting. The poetry resolutely enacts a lack of resolution, a fearless fearfulness. The tensings in these lines can be readily appreciated if heard against Eliot's earlier attempt:

> At the violet hour, the hour when eyes and back and hand
> Turn upward from the desk, the human engine waits –
> Like a taxi throbbing waiting at a stand –[13]

The 'hand/stand' rhyme denies the throbbingly intense incompletion of 'throbbing waiting'; and the way in which a simple excision has raised the merely descriptive 'waiting at a stand' to emotional intensity is a minor triumph. As Eliot knew, there is an art of deliberate and close repetition:[14] in the final text the two 'throbbings' do not merely throb with repetition, for the first stresses the mechanicalness of the alienated 'human engine', which exists in terms of its parts, its 'eye' and 'back' and so on, while the second reinvests the human engine with 'throbbing' humanity. Passion and horror of passion mingle in that phrase 'throbbing between two lives': Tiresias is torn 'between two lives' in his mythically bi-sexual state, and he also sympathetically throbs with the life that is 'between' the two sexes.

These nine lines constitute one of the most astonishing in Eliot's considerable repertoire of syntactical feats. Their single sentence proceeds surreptitiously, catching the reader off guard. We 'wait' for a resolution, which is waiveringly proffered and then withdrawn in a state of grammatically suspended animation. The troubled status of Tiresias as 'seer' comes across in a troubled syntax, at once sinuous and uncertain. 'Though blind', Tiresias 'can see', but it is not clear grammatically what he does see. 'Can see', the main verb, comes at the end of the sentence's fifth line, after which, at the turn of the line, comes a repetition of the introductory adverbial phrase 'At the violet hour', a taking of breath in anticipation of whatever it is that Tiresias can see, which at first seems to be 'the typist'. But in that case, as Donald Davie has pointed out, 'there is no subject for the next verbs, no one left to clear the breakfast, light the stove, lay out tins'. One way round this difficulty is to hear the verb 'can see' as intransitive, as not having any specific object of sight, so that '*what* Tiresias sees, in fact', turns out to be hazy. In this reading it can be 'the evening hour' that clears the breakfast and so on.[15]

The effect of this grammatical slipperiness is, again, to focus attention as much on Tiresias's consciousness as on what he is conscious of. Involved and distant, by turns he experiences and spurns the emotions he describes. An equivocal visionary, he has a Tennysonian lassitude, more specifically the horrified boredom of Tennyson's Tithonus, who, like Ovid's Tiresias, was granted the doubtful gift of everlasting life. Ennui, 'foresuffering all', tugs against anticipation. He both participates in the lives of others, and is empty of life. Just as the 'hour' governs the figures in this human comedy, so time traps Tiresias in its continuum. His second self-declaration lays more emphasis on the waiting and less on the throbbing:

> I Tiresias, old man with wrinkled dugs
> Perceived the scene, and foretold the rest –
> I too awaited the expected guest.

These lines are tonally unplaceable. Tedium mingles with expectation. Seeing has given way to 'perceiving', which is a mental as well as visual act. Tiresias here mingles the role of voyeur with that of world-weary satirist. His foretelling shifts from the oracular to the tone of one who 'has seen it all before'. He awaits the guest with a slightly scornful sense of the inevitable, the scorn audible in the arch 'awaited' (instead of 'waited for'), and the archer 'expected guest'.

Tiresias's prophetic credentials are voyeuristically inserted into the narrative between parentheses:

> His vanity requires no response,
> And makes a welcome of indifference.
> (And I Tiresias have foresuffered all
> Enacted on this same divan or bed;
> I who have sat by Thebes below the wall
> And walked among the lowest of the dead.)
> Bestows one final patronising kiss,
> And gropes his way, finding the stairs unlit...

The grammatical subject of 'Bestows' is shifting and shifty. At first it seems to carry over from the sentence preceding the parenthesis: 'His vanity' bestows the kiss. But it must be the clerk, not his vanity, who 'gropes his way' in the next line, so that retrospectively the reader makes the clerk the subject of 'Bestows'. From one point of view it makes no difference, since his vanity belongs to him. But from another it makes all the difference: he is so taken over by his vanity as to become indistinguishable from it, so that his individuality is submerged in his ruling emotion. (Eliot may have learnt this literary lesson from Dante, though of course the lesson is much more than literary.) In the original version in quatrains the parenthesis constituted a complete stanza, so that the reader's eye separated it off as an evident hiatus. But in the final text the parenthesis appears less separable, more a part of the re-'enactment' in the present of this age-old act; and Tiresias sounds as though he may be coming out of his parentheses, as though he too may be getting involved in the subject of 'bestows'. The troubled syntax enacts his 'foresuffering'.[16]

The Waste Land's Tiresias combines elements of Ovid's and Sophocles's, and, not to miss his Classical cues, Eliot also gestures at the Tiresias whom Odysseus meets in the Underworld in *Odyssey II*. But even as the casual liaison of typist and clerk is opened up to tragic and epic perspectives, the poetry seems incredulous of its own allusive manoeuvres: to 'have sat by Thebes below the wall' sounds like a casual way of putting it; and the epic dignity of 'And walked among the lowest of the dead' is compromised if we recollect the different use of 'low' thirteen lines earlier, in 'One of the low on whom assurance sits'. Tiresias's ear is attuned, like that of his ventriloquial creator, the *émigré* American, to gradations of spoken English. He betrays an English disdain, incongruous from the mouth of a prophet of antiquity. But then incongruity is a hallmark of *The Waste Land*. This prophet speaks eighteenth-century poetic pastiche, with affected inversion ('the young man carbunclar'), pedantry (most of us would say, more colloquially, 'like a silk hat', not 'as a silk hat'), pernickety phrasing ('as he guesses'), and stand-offish diction ('Endeavours to engage her in caresses').

But the condescending air can modulate into ironic pathos, particularly in relation to the typist. Satire mixes with sadness in 'Out of the window perilously spread / Her drying combinations touched by the sun's last rays': 'perilously' blends comedy with a hint of her perilous situation. A similar effect is audible in the fleeting but ironic merging of the typist with Olivia, heroine of Goldsmith's *The Vicar of Wakefield*. In Olivia's song, the famous first line of which Eliot has distorted, she grieves for her seduction in lines that full-throatedly 'soothe her melancholy' even as she bemoans her lack of 'art' to do so. The song adds to the growing number of muted voices of wronged women that allusively haunt *The Waste Land*:

> When lovely woman stoops to folly
> And finds too late that men betray
> What charm can soothe her melancholy,
> What art can wash her guilt away?
>
> The only art her guilt to cover,
> To hide her shame from every eye,
> To give repentance to her lover
> And wring his bosom – is to die.

But, unlike the words of Ophelia echoed at the end of 'A Game of Chess', Olivia's do not in fact signify death, for she does not pine away; and, in the way of novels of 'sentiment', in the end she turns out to be legally married to the man who thought he had wronged her. Eliot's 'art' unsoothingly punctures Olivia's sentimental melancholy, to be sure; but he replaces it not, as may at first seem to be the case, with mere scorn for his modern heroine's spiritual vacuity (Olivia, after all, anxious for many lovers, may be a lively character, but she is not remarkable for spiritual depth), but with a numbed sense of hopelessness, a realisation of blocked emotion more trenchant than anything Goldsmith was capable of:

> When lovely woman stoops to folly and
> Paces about her room again, alone,
> She smoothes her hair with automatic hand,
> And puts a record on the gramophone.

Ricks writes that Eliot sabotages Goldsmith's line by 'undoing it by adding the innocuous little word "and" ', which is true but not the whole truth.[17] Eliot makes Goldsmith's line sound off-key by moving the innocuous little word back from the start of Goldsmith's second line to the end of his first. This is undoing Goldsmith's line so as to re-do it, for Eliot has deftly turned an iambic tetrameter into an iambic pentameter merely by shifting the innocuous one-syllable word. Goldsmith's first line, and every alternate line, is a tetrameter with an extra syllable at the end. This syllable creates a dying and melancholy fall; these 'feminine' endings fade away as our heroine is supposed to be doing. Turning Goldsmith's line into a pentameter gives to its wistfulness a questioningly acerbic edge – questioningly because the added 'and' is unassertive; it unsteadies the rhythm of the line without asserting a new one. From here Eliot's lines can shift into the surer pentametric irony of 'She smoothes her hair with automatic hand / And puts a record on the gramophone.' The melodrama of Olivia's remorse contrasts with the absence of drama, the remorselessness, of the 'automatic hand'. But even as Eliot's lines suppress the lyric voice, its importunity can be felt. The phrase 'her departed lover' is plainly ironic, but it acknowledges the possibility of what is absent. What is choked back signifies as much as what breaks into strangulated utterance, the sadly jaunty 'Well now that's done: and I'm glad it's over.'

After the gramophone, a pause, and then 'This music crept

by me upon the waters'. This switch is remarkable for its combination of the arbitrary- and the inevitable-sounding. It hints at the auditory procedures of *The Waste Land*. The line both listens to what has just been happening in the poem and anticipates what is to come. It intimates *The Waste Land*'s musical interplay, the way the poetry proceeds by vocal adjustments and juxtapositions.[18] The line, from the episode in *The Tempest* I. ii where Ferdinand enters following Ariel's song, triggers both immediate and more general associations. Perhaps the least interesting aspect is the Shakespearian thematic web which commentators are fond of describing: watery grave and possible rebirth. More interesting is the effect of the transition from the gramophone to 'this music'. If the music is, momentarily at least, that of the gramophone, then Ferdinand's word 'crept' is being gently mocked. But 'this music' also anticipates 'The pleasant whining of a mandoline' four lines later. It conjures up as well all the different musics in 'The Fire Sermon' associated with water, the song of Spenser's 'Prothalamion', the soda-water song about Mrs Porter and her daughter, and the Song of the Thames-daughters which is to come (lines 266 ff.).

In what way the Song of the Thames-daughters 'creeps' by, whether or not pleasantly, is not easy to determine. According to Eliot's note his Thames-daughters elide with the Rhine-daughters of *Götterdämmerung* III. i, and Stefan Hawlin, in his article on Eliot's reading of *The Waste Land*, argues that 'Eliot has written his lyric over his memory of the total atmosphere' of *Götterdämmerung* III. i. He continues:

> The music reinforces the mixed joy and sadness of [Wagner's] words, for on the one hand it enacts the memory of the gold shining beautifully in the sunlight, on the other the sense of its loss. Eliot's lyric is similarly divided, celebratory of the Thames yet also sensing it to be a casualty of the waste land. The expansive song of the Rhine maidens is cut back to something terse. In *Götterdämmerung* ... the flowing motif runs on and on: 'Wei-a-la---la, wei-a la---la lei-a lei-a wal-la-la------la lei---a la la lei---la la la' (bars 97–102, and continuing), but this reduces to 'Weialala leia / Wallala leialala'.... He performs it

> quickly and rhythmically in the recording, so shutting down on the lyrical fullness that it might otherwise seem to suggest. Like other allusions it is not, firstly, a piece of knowledge set down to build up the mythos of the poem (as one could believe from paraphrases) but rather a sensuously remembered fragment lodged in the mind through its phonic qualities and only then adapted to its context.[19]

This is a timely reminder that the motive for much of *The Waste Land*'s allusiveness is auditory, and at the same time, paradoxically, that how we hear the poem is frequently unclear. The Song of the Thames-daughters, 'cut back to something terse', suggesting indeed a 'shutting down on ... lyrical fullness', does nevertheless compose a skeletal music fuller than that of other female voices in *The Waste Land*. In Spenser's 'Prothalamion' the stream 'murmurde low, / As he would speak' in sympathy with the singing of the Nymphs, 'but that he lackt a tong'. Here in *The Waste Land* the Song of the Thames-daughters is nothing like as full as that of Spenser's Nymphs, to be sure, but at least they have found a voice more articulate than the violated and tongueless Philomel's with her 'Twit twit twit / Jug jug jug ...'. It sounds 'divided' between the strangulated and something more singing. Though the lines are very short, they are set off by pronounced, if irregular, rhyming; they struggle into lyrical utterance. The relationship between the contemporary Thames of the Song's first section (lines 266–78) and the Elizabethan Thames of the second (lines 279–91) is indefinable. Neither the poetry nor Eliot's note quoting from his source for the river tryst between Elizabeth I and the Earl of Leicester supports Hawlin's forthright conclusion that 'Elizabethan London repeats the present, and nothing changes.'[20] The relationship between Eliot's music and his predecessors' is much less certain than that. As so often with *The Waste Land*'s art of allusion, evocation of the past alerts poet and reader alike to the dangers of nostalgia. Just how sceptical should we be of Spenser's full-throated verbal music?

'Cutting back to something terse' and 'shutting down on ... lyrical fullness' are even more in evidence when the Thames-daughters speak in turn (lines 292–306). The 'music' is now that of tight-lipped speech, bitter with all that goes unsaid. Lines fragment, line-endings break up short sentences ('Richmond and Kew / Undid me.'; 'After the event / He wept.'), and whole lines consist of sentence-heads ('Trams and dusty trees.'; 'On Margate Sands.'; 'The broken finger-nails of dirty hands.'). The scoring in verse of these intonations is a triumph of originality. Yet these daughters of the flood speak in a way, concise but emotionally revealing, colloquial but with an underspoken dignity, which, as a note by Eliot hints, owes much to his reading of Dante:

> 'Trams and dusty trees.
> Highbury bore me. Richmond and Kew
> Undid me. By Richmond I raised my knees
> Supine on the floor of a narrow canoe.'

As Eliot's note indicates, 'undid' is a translation of 'disfecemi' in the line spoken by La Pia at the end of *Purgatorio* V, 'Siena mi fe', disfecemi Maremma', which the Temple Classics edition translates as 'Siena made me, Maremma unmade me.' But Eliot has made Dante's line uniquely his own. The Italian reads like an epitaph denoting lineage by place of birth and death, but it plays acerbically on the convention with its 'made–unmade' antithesis: Siena is the place of her birth, but Maremma is the place not merely of her death; Maremma is the place where she was unmade, done to death, murdered. Eliot's first Thames-daughter sounds like a soul speaking from the dead, but she has been 'undone' in a different way. Her undoing gives rise to some bitter verbal wit at her own expense, in the word 'supine' – if indeed the wit is not more than verbal: Dante's dead assume physical attitudes which denote their spiritual state. However, the edgy language of Eliot's Thames-daughter is anything but 'supine'.

This is not the 'automatic' speech of the 'Well now that's done: and I'm glad it's over' variety. The three Thames-daughters describe their undoings in terms of bodily parts – 'knees', 'feet', 'heart', 'hands' – in a kind of numbed and pained anatomical synecdoche. They have become unsettlingly dispersed and subordinated. 'My feet are at Moorgate, and my heart / Under my feet': this is emotional derangement speaking with chilling matter-of-factness. The place-names of Highbury, Richmond, Kew, Moorgate, Margate, do not 'place' the Thames-daughters, give them lineage and identity, as Siena and Maremma do for La Pia; rather they displace them, drain them of identity. The names even set up their own ghostly kind of 'music' in the distant chiming of Margate with Moorgate. The poet enables the daughters to utter their emotional emptiness with finely tuned lack of cadence: 'I made no comment. What should I resent?' That line is another of Eliot's studies in flat speaking. Depending on which of the last four words you stress, you get four different senses; or you can read them without any stress. It is impossible to tell if the emotional emptiness comes from stunned emotions, or inadequate emotions. The level tone denotes level-headedness; or it denotes empty-headedness: holding it all back, or having nothing to hold back. The words of the third Thames-daughter are similarly disoriented and disorienting. Her 'people' may 'expect / Nothing', but what she makes of her inheritance is less certain: 'I can connect / Nothing with nothing', not 'I cannot connect anything with anything.' This does not sound like the 'nothing' of the hyacinth garden, the 'no thing' that is positively 'known'. But is there not audible a possibility of recovery in those words 'I can connect', set off as they are in their own line? Is there not here, working against the void, an effort to make connections, a resilience, a starting again at the beginning? The desire to find voices for these women of 'The Fire Sermon', to make the violated inviolable, testifies not only to the poet's guilt perhaps, but also to his effort to atone – at the deepest level, in the poetry.

Lyrical fullness is even more severely 'shut down on' with the syllables 'la la', presumably chanted by all three Thames-daughters again briefly ensemble – although so severely and so briefly that the syllables sound equally like an ironically distanced interjection, a musical throwing up of the hands, so to speak, almost a 'tra la la'. Irresolution hovers too over the final lines of 'The Fire Sermon'. They begin confidently – 'To

Carthage then I came' – as if rounding things off by coming at them from a different angle, in the manner of a musical coda, that is, 'a passage added after the natural completion of a movement, so as to form a more definite and satisfactory conclusion' (in the words of the OED). Eliot's note reproduces more of the allusion to St Augustine's *Confessions*: 'to Carthage then I came, where a cauldron of unholy loves sang all about mine ears.'[21] Heard in the context of this fuller quotation, does the allusion to St Augustine signify dismissal of the Thames-daughters' Song and their monologues as the sounds of unholy loves singing all about our and the poet's ears? But the allusion to unholy singing loves is not in the poem itself. The vatic note continues with the line 'Burning burning burning burning', words which are apparently taken from the Buddha's Fire Sermon, although we would not know it but for Eliot's note. We begin to wonder whether and how much we are being encouraged to read into the lines, and whether there is not some leg-pulling going on – as much at the poem's as at the reader's expense. The lines 'O Lord Thou pluckest me out / O Lord Thou pluckest / burning' gain an apocalyptic and prophetic strain from their alluding not only to the *Confessions* again, to St Augustine's divine rescue from sensual temptation (Eliot's note points out the allusion), but possibly also to the words of the prophets Amos and Zechariah about sinners and non-believers being firebrands plucked from the fire.[22] But how is the truncated repetition 'O Lord Thou pluckest' to be registered? Do the last lines of 'The Fire Sermon' shorten tauteningly as they strain towards the incandescent concluding monosyllable, 'burning'? Or do they falter forward in a diminuendo, hardly making it to that final, isolated syllable before petering out? Does 'The Fire Sermon' end with a bang or a whimper? Does the prophetic strain fail to ring true, or does the poetry acknowledge this and deflate its own portentousness? The absence of punctuation in the last six lines, the space surrounding some of them, the final word suspended and syntactically floating, mean that what was indefinite and unsatisfactory as a conclusion ('la la') is followed by something equally as indefinite and unsatisfactory, by a sort of anti-coda. But then this may be what is required: not definiteness and satisfaction but a sense of auditory suspension and unresolved cadence, of irresolution, that nothing is closed or decided.

IV

'Death by Water'

In contrast to some of the other oracular passages in *The Waste Land*, 'Death by Water' sounds authoritative. But the authority came as an afterthought. With this section of the poem Eliot alluded not only to the vast treasurehouse of the literature of the past, but also to the smaller treasurehouse of his own literary output of the recent past: a near-translation of his French poem 'Dans le Restaurant', it was originally tacked on to the end of a deliberately written sea-voyage-cum-fishing-expedition. This narrative, which Eliot remembered as being 'rather inspired' by the account of Ulysses's last voyage at the end of *Inferno* XXVI, does not match up to Dante's 'well-told seaman's yarn', as Eliot was to call it.[1] The excised narrative includes an ancient-mariner-like vision of Sirens, who are a nightmarish version of the singing mermaids in 'The Love Song of J. Alfred Prufrock'. In particular, the end is reminiscent of the last sentence of Dante's account:

> Tre volte il fe' girar con tutte l'acque,
> all quarta levar la poppa in suso,
> e la prora ire in giù com' altrui piacque,
> infin che il mar fu sopra noi richiuso.

(Three times it made her whirl round with all the waters; at the fourth, made the poop rise up and prow go down, as pleased Another, till the sea was closed above us.)

(*Inferno* XXVI. 139–42)

The only recollection of these lines to remain in Eliot's final text is the line 'Entering the whirlpool'. But in the original sea narrative Dante's 'Another' also made an appearance, at the conclusion of the voyage and immediately preceding the lines about Phlebas: 'And if *Another* knows, I know I know not, / Who only know that there is no more noise now.' Dante's lines remind us of how his Ulysses is different from Homer's. Homer's is nostalgic: he journeys home. Dante's, with his insatiable and heroic hunger for knowledge and experience, abjures the nostalgic comforts of home and is damned for pride: he and his companions are shipwrecked by the storm that blows from the very place of their destination, the 'montagna bruna' (l. 133), the Mount of Purgatory. Dante's Ulysses thus gains the knowledge of damnation already implicit in his proud search, and experiences God, or 'Another' (for, as John D. Sinclair remarks, 'God cannot be named by the lost'),[2] only at the moment of damnation. Eliot's excised lines combine the two emotions of nostalgia and pride. At the moment of going under, his narrator is made to say, with unlikely bravado, 'Home and mother. / Where's a cocktail shaker, Ben, here's plenty of cracked ice. / Remember me.'[3]

Eliot deeply re-thought and re-felt 'Dans le Restaurant' in translating it for its new context. In the French poem Phlebas forgot not only the profit and loss but also 'the Cornish swell' and 'the cargo of tin': 'la houle de Cornouaille, / Et les profits et les pertes, et la cargaison d'étain'. Here the profit and loss are specific, related to a particular trade. In 'Death by Water' they become general and elegiac – though they are still related, be it indirectly, to trade through association with Phoenicia, a seafaring and trading nation, and more indirectly still through references to trade elsewhere in *The Waste Land* ('the one-eyed merchant', 'Mr. Eugenides, the Smyrna merchant'; and the Punic Wars, which appear in the line 'You who were with me in the ships at Mylae!', were about trade). In 'Death by Water' the profit and loss imply a universal moral balance sheet weighing all that we are and could be.

'Dans le Restaurant' does not contain the whirlpool:

> Un courant de sous-mer l'emporta très loin,
> Le repassant aux étapes de sa vie antérieure.

(A current undersea carried him very far, making him pass through the stages of his former life.)

In 'Death by Water' this becomes:

> A current under sea
> Picked his bones in whispers. As he rose and fell
> He passed the stages of his age and youth
> Entering the whirlpool.

Dante's great emblem of ultimate hope and despair, Ulysses passing the threshold of mortal limits and getting sucked under within sight of Purgatory 'as pleased Another', lies behind Eliot's whirlpool, which takes on a universal significance absent from 'Dans le Restaurant'. At the same time Dante's whirlpool has been interiorised and given psychological intensity, has become the psyche's interior swirl encountering and re-living past emotional experience.

The alteration in the action of the undersea current, from 'l'emporta très loin' to 'Picked his bones in whispers', is inspired. In a compelling essay (in the form of a dialogue) on the richly allusive texture of 'Dans le Restaurant', William Arrowsmith writes:

> In *The Waste Land*, Phlebas' death is linked to the sea-change music of Shakespeare's *Tempest*, and thence to all the other water-musics of the poem, to Wagner's *Tristran and Isolde*, Spenser's *Prothalamion*, the Rhine-maidens, and so on.

By contrast, argues Arrowsmith, 'Dans le Restaurant' lacks this sense of rich sea-change:

> The important fact is pain; and the pain is emphasized, rather strongly for Eliot, by a whole line: 'Figurez-vous donc, c'était un sort pénible.' In the 'Death by Water' sequence of *The Waste Land*, the emphasis is unmistakably on the gentleness of Phlebas' death ('A current under sea / Picked his bones in whispers.'). Now if you echo *The Tempest*, you're certain to end up stressing the mildness – gentled by imagination and metaphor – of death by drowning.[4]

This is true. 'Un sort pénible', a painful fate, does not appear in 'Death by Water'. Yet the 'gentleness' comes with a hint of Gothic horror. The sea current picks at the bones with a conspiratorial fastidiousness, 'in whispers'. The effect is spookily assuaging. Fascination and horror, compulsion and revulsion, mingle in Eliot's music of sea-change. This double sense is conveyed with brilliant succinctness in 'Entering the whirlpool'. Even as that phrase conjures up the fate of Dante's Ulysses, it distances itself from it, for Dante's Ulysses is sucked involuntarily under, whereas Eliot's Phlebas partly welcomes his end: he 'enters' actively, participating even after death.

V

'What the Thunder said'

Many critics, encouraged no doubt by Eliot's statement that 'the final section of the poem remained exactly as I first wrote it', feel that with 'What the Thunder said' *The Waste Land* at last breaks through to an authentic and whole voice.[1] Confirmation of this view comes from the fact that Eliot said he was describing his own experience of composing this section when he wrote in his essay 'The "Pensées" of Pascal' (1931) that

> it is a commonplace that some forms of illness are extremely favourable, not only to religious illumination, but to artistic and literary composition. A piece of writing meditated, apparently without progress, for months or years, may suddenly take shape and word; and in this state long passages may be produced which require little or no retouch.[2]

But even though for much of the time the writing sounds more fluent than in previous sections, the voice of 'What the Thunder said' is far from unequivocal and univocal. As for Eliot's tricky elision of 'religious illumination' and 'literary composition', that warrants further comment, especially in relation to the end of the poem.

The title itself, 'What the Thunder said', riddlingly plays with the oracular. More resonantly and insistently oracular are the opening lines. Indeed, at the third 'After' we begin to wonder if the poetry is not becoming too obviously sonorous; but even as we start to ask if it can sustain itself thus, it begins possibly not to. As Ricks has shown, uncertainty about how to hear the lines increases. Are we to supply an 'After' also at the start of the fourth and fifth lines, which thus build to a syntactical crescendo at the seventh line; or does the crescendo come earlier? In this 'syntactical dubiety', writes Ricks,

> The sequence is clear as to each unit of meaning but not as to its articulate energy. Is it a series of lines that stretches out to the crack of doom, the doom finally arrived at as 'He who was living is now dead'? . . . Or is the voice to arrive earlier? After that, and that, and that, then this, this, this.

This uncertainty prepares for subsequent equivocation:

> He who was living is now dead
> We who were living are now dying
> With a little patience

Ricks asks: 'Is the antithesis finished at "dying"? But then "dying" has not arrived at the endedness of "dead".... Is "With a little patience" a retrospect or a prospect?' The lines refuse to 'placate our impatience and settle the matter: no full stop after "dying" or after "patience"'.[3] Depending on whether one stops after the unpunctuated word 'dying' or reads on into the next line conveys either a new beginning and hope, or a diminuendo of hopelessness. In the space that succeeds these open-ended opening lines the reader is suspended between 'living' and 'dying', between hopefulness and hopelessness. But the lines do not dither, though they equivocate. They enact patience, the sense of what it feels like not to know the outcome.

The ensuing 'water-dripping song' (lines 331–58), as Eliot called it, the only passage he excepted from his feeling, expressed shortly after composing *The Waste Land*, that the poem was 'ephemeral', extends patience into what Ricks calls its 'companions': 'endurance, fortitude and perseverance'.[4] C. K. Stead writes that these lines 'with their repetitions ("rock" eight [*sic*] times, "water" eleven times, "mountains" five times in twenty-eight lines) can seem thin'.[5] But this is another instance, and a supreme one, of Eliot's art of deliberate and close repetition. The first half of the song is very different from the second, and the repetitions do not produce a uniform effect. In the first half, they 'can seem', on the contrary, to have a thickening effect; in the second, their effect is a thinning in the sense, not of a dissipation of intensity, but, on the contrary, of a sharpening, a honing to the thinness of acuity ('If there were the sound of water *only*').

In the first half, that is, for fifteen lines, the poetry sounds as though it is standing still even as it moves forward:

> Here is no water but only rock
> Rock and no water and the sandy road
> The road winding above among the mountains
> Which are mountains of rock without water

This is a thickening of: 'Here is no water but only rock and the sandy road winding above, among the mountains', which is a satisfyingly articulate skeleton of a sentence. The fleshed-out version is not more, but less supple. For the fifteen lines there is nothing that sounds like a caesura. Even where one is expected, between 'above' and 'among' in the line 'The road winding above among the mountains', there is none. Since none of the lines are punctuated, talk of end-stopped and run-on lines is beside the point, although it is possible to say that sometimes the syntax resumes after a line-break, as in the lines just quoted, and that sometimes it starts again, as at the beginning of each of the next four lines:

> If there were water we should stop and drink
> Amongst the rock one cannot stop or think
> Sweat is dry and feet are in the sand
> If there were only water amongst the rock

But word pattern and repetition, all the auditory effects of this poetry, take precedence over the stoppings and startings of conventional syntax. It is a new sound in English poetry. The lines do not move with suppleness; they toil stiffly on. It is not merely a matter of taking one step back at the start of each line ('*rock* / *Rock*', '*road* / The *road*', '*mountains* / Which are *mountains*); the second line of the song takes two steps back ('no *water* but only *rock* / *Rock* and no *water*'), and the fourth retreats through all the steps of 'mountains', 'rock' and 'water' right back to the beginning. The poetry enacts the agony of going round in solipsistic circles: 'my experience falls within my own circle.'

Yet stiffness is allied to stiffening, and the poetry is intense with effort, with the labour of the mind trying to climb out of itself. When we say a poem is laboured we usually mean it is bad. Eliot's lines transform labour into incantation: 'Dead mountain mouth of carious teeth that cannot spit / Here one can neither stand nor lie nor sit'. Heard out of context these lines approach doggerel. The dogged rhythm, the plodding rhyme ('nor sit' sounds like a dogged determination not to forgo the rhyme of yet another denied posture), and the elaboration of the mountain-teeth analogy (not just mountains that look like teeth, not just, therefore, a mouth of mountains, and not just teeth that are carious because the mountain is dead, but a mountain-mouth that cannot spit), have meaning only as they convey the determination not to give up against the steep odds. The poetic art of endurance entails also the ability to keep a cadence going beyond expectations and beyond endurance:

> There is not even silence in the mountains
> But dry sterile thunder without rain
> There is not even solitude in the mountains
> But red sullen faces sneer and snarl
> From doors of mudcracked houses

The first 'But' means 'apart from' and does not anticipate a subordinate clause containing a verb. Because of the 'There is not even silence' / 'There is not even solitude' parallelism, the second 'But' initially reads like the first to mean 'apart from', but the appearance of the verbs 'sneer and snarl' turns the second 'But' into the start of a subordinate clause more elaborate than expected. The lines go on that bit longer than they sounded as though they would. They do not easily win through to a resolving cadence, but they do not let up; they persevere.

Whether in fact they do win through is not determinable. Two of the repeated words in the second half of the water-dripping song, 'water' and 'rock', are the same as in the first half. But now the repetitions modulate from insistent incantation into lines that begin to sound, hesitantly, as though they want to sing:

> If there were water
> And no rock
> If there were rock
> And also water
> And water
> A spring
> A pool among the rock

– and the lines lengthen into the realisation of the beautiful and seemingly more assured cadence of:

> Where the hermit-thrush sings in the pine trees
> Drip drop drip drop drop drop drop

'But', of course, 'there is no water': the poetry catches itself off guard. In a sense, though, the water is there, in the poetry's soundings, drip-dropping with refreshing cadence. The dwelling on 'water' and on the 'sound of water' challenges its absence, overriding the repeated conditional ('If there were') of its presence. The water is there for a lyrical moment. The syllables 'Drip drop drip drop drop drop drop' deny those other syllables 'Twit twit twit / Jug jug jug jug jug jug'. 'But there is no water'; after those watery sounds the disappointment is acute.

'In the first part of Part V three themes are employed': it is as much the concept of themes as the flat assurance with which Eliot's note goes on to list them that raises an eyebrow. '[T]he present decay of eastern Europe' is summary to the point of perfunctory. Stead is right to resist: 'though there is a chapel referred to, we would scarcely see it as the Chapel Perilous of the legends without the prompting of the note. The Chapel Perilous is in the notes to the poem but it is not strictly in the poem.' But perhaps Stead's suspicions should extend to the rhetoric of the poem itself. He praises the two paragraphs beginning 'What is that sound high in the air' and 'A woman drew her long black hair out tight' for possessing, 'in the sheer poetic force with which the negative iterations are made, an inevitable affirmative charge, a note of triumph, of mastery'. But is there not something spuriously apocalyptic in poetry containing such phrases as 'hooded hordes swarming', 'stumbling in cracked earth', 'the city over the mountains / Cracks and reforms and bursts in the violet air', and in these lines:

> A woman drew her long black hair out tight
> And fiddled whisper music on those strings
> And bats with baby faces in the violet light
> Whistled, and beat their wings
> And crawled head downward down a blackened wall
> And upside down in air were towers
> Tolling reminiscent bells, that kept the hours
> And voices singing out of empty cisterns and exhausted wells.

'Verbal magnificence', writes Stead.[6] The lines do a magnificent job of getting away with some obvious verbal effects. Six 'and's maintain the momentum. Is the word 'long' present other than for the rhythm (it would be difficult to draw out short hair)? '[H]ead downward down . . . / And upside down' orchestrates an impressive verbal plunge, but the words 'head downward' are, strictly speaking, superfluous. 'And towers were upside down in air' would be the more natural word order, but Eliot's order allows not only the 'towers/hours' rhyme but also a high-flown out-of-the-ordinariness. The lines are not 'speaking strictly', of course. As has often been noted, they achieve an impressive surreality; but perhaps such an effect necessitates redundancy and the patently high-flown. How much is the voice of this poetry itself singing out of an exhausted well, so that to achieve its effects it has to over-achieve them?

The lines toll in a way that sounds 'reminiscent'. ' "Murmur of maternal lamentation" ', writes Stead, 'could not have been bettered by Tennyson', which is true; but then why out-Tennyson Tennyson in 1922?[7] The language draws attention to itself. 'The link between the hooded figure of the road to Emmaus and the "hooded hordes swarming" is not much more than verbal', writes Leavis; but not much less, either.[8] Again Stead writes, 'Ganga, Himavant, DA – the magical words embedded like gems in the fabric are an essential part of the rhetoric, just as they are in Coleridge's "In Xanadu did Kubla Khan..."', which rightly resists the temptation to reduce *The Waste Land* to paraphrase.[9] But is the verbal magic unambiguously attractive? Is there not something meretricious in its gleam?

In particular, what sort of spell does 'DA', voice of the thunder, cast? It sounds out of a difficult silence: 'The jungle crouched, humped in silence'. The defensive-aggressive posture of 'crouched' becomes stubbornly inscrutable with 'humped' – which is the posture of the whole of *The Waste Land*, inviting and warding off interpretative attacks. The thunder is announced by a flourish of inversion: 'Then spoke the thunder'. 'DA' has undergone much scrutiny, but the opposed responses it has inspired confirm the inscrutability. It is the voice of oracular authority or of sibylline irresponsibility. It signifies primal unity or ultimate fragmentation, prelapsarian wholeness or postlapsarian disintegration, fullness of utterance or vacuity of utterance, the beginning or the end. It has elicited the unlearned response (thunder sounds like DA) and the learned. The latter has to do with the fact that 'DA' is the root syllable of three not just foreign, but (to most readers) unfamilar words, but which Eliot's note reveals to be Sanskrit, from one of the *Upanishads*. Some of the critical response to 'DA' and the Sanskrit words deserve further examination, but meanwhile what sort of response do they get in the poem itself? –

> *Datta:* what have we given?
> My friend, blood shaking my heart
> The awful daring of a moment's surrender
> Which an age of prudence can never retract
> By this, and this only, we have existed

These words sound intimate – 'My friend', not, for instance, 'mon semblable' – but they are also riddling. The intensely private self, 'not to be found in our obituaries / Or in memories draped by the beneficent spider' (words that finely capture the saving but falsifying deceptions exercised by time), is confirmed by the language in which it expresses itself. At the moment of comprehending the agony of solipsism the language ensnares itself more deeply in it. The line 'By this, and this only, we have existed' equivocates absolutely. Patient beyond words, it allows of no possibility of resolution. 'Only' is a little word on which a lot turns. 'And this only' is either a diminution ('only' meaning merely: 'this mere moment is all we have of significance to show for our lives') or an intensification ('only' meaning solely, uniquely: 'our lives are significant only by virtue of this supreme moment'); or rather it is both, the language holding in tense relationship two opposed attitudes, straining at each other. Diminution and intensification threaten to cancel each other out; entrapment tangles with release, enslavement with freedom; in religious terms, damnation with redemption. Hence 'The awful daring of a moment's surrender' is inscrutably Janus-faced. 'Awful' is a word that looks both ways. One can either be defeated by dwelling on such intense memories, or be redeemed through them, as with the key that can both lock and unlock a few lines later. *The Waste Land*'s 'moment' is a decisive turning-point, but nothing has been decided. The only decisive thing is the firmness of the indecision: patience and fortitude again.

These lines turn on syntactic ambiguity:

> *Dayadhvam:* I have heard the key
> Turn in the door once and turn once only
> We think of the key, each in his prison
> Thinking of the key, each confirms a prison
> Only at nightfall, aethereal rumours
> Revive for a moment a broken Coriolanus

A tense conjunction of opposites enacts the difficulty of breaking out of solipsism. The key that locks up, isolates, is the same key that unlocks, that offers liberation and emotional contact; which is to say, understanding the reason for isolation offers the possibility of escape from isolation. The syntax is locked in on itself, imprisoned; it is difficult to break out of the phrasing. 'Each in his prison' attaches grammatically both to the previous phrase ('We think of the key') and to the subsequent one ('Thinking of the key'), depending on whether one reads through the unpunctuated line ending or halts at it. 'Thinking of the key' similarly refers grammatically backward and forward, and so do the two subsequent half-lines, 'each confirms a prison' and 'Only at nightfall'. In each case the line-ending can be heard as both a turning-point and a stopping-point. But the lines do not dither; they enact a resolute uncertainty. The harder one tries to escape from this labyrinth of language, the more locked in one becomes, the more the 'prison' is confirmed. But release is also audible. The line 'We think of the key, each in his prison', heard as a single unit of sense, closes the door, intimating the isolation of each of us. But then 'each in his prison / Thinking of the key', heard as another unit, opens the door, because for one isolated individual to think of the isolation of another momentarily breaks through the wall of isolation: *Dayadhvam* means sympathise, according to Eliot's note. But then the line 'Thinking of the key, each confirms a prison', read as another unit, closes the door again, while 'each confirms a prison / Only at nightfall' opens it once more, if only ajar: nightfall brings shades of the prison-house, but daylight brings. . . . But then begin again at 'Only at nightfall' and read through to 'a broken Coriolanus', and you end up with something highly equivocal: night brings on the temptation to dream oneself as an undefeated Coriolanus, but his stature depended on self-possession, the inability or refusal to break out of the prison-house of self, on lack of sympathy. This is a hollow revival. The lines are extraordinarily self-possessed in expressing, in refusing to duck, the agony of equivocation; they are patiently possessed by the intransigence of their emotions.[10]

'Turn in the door once and turn once only': turning is an Eliotic obsession. 'La Figlia Che Piange' is possessed by a moment of turning, an emotional turn and a turn in a relationship, as the poem returns to a memory it would turn away from. It turns on its consciousness of the girl's 'turning away', which is proposed in the first verse-paragraph and remembered in the last: proposed as something desired or regretted – it is impossible to tell which, for the poem mixes the two emotions – but not as something that necessarily took place in the way it returns to the memory ('So I would have had him leave, / So I would have had her stand . . .'). Even as she more certainly 'turns away' in the last verse-paragraph, she does so only to 'compel' the 'imagination' into the present, which continues to revolve how things would have turned out ('And I wonder how they should have been together!') if events had taken a different turn. 'Burnt Norton' is able to spell out what 'La Figlia Che Piange' was working out:

> What might have been is an abstraction
> Remaining a perpetual possibility
> Only in a world of speculation.
> What might have been and what has been
> Point to one end, which is always present.

(Again the word 'only' signifies both diminution and intensification, 'merely' and 'solely'.) Every moment is therefore a turning-point, the intersection of past and future, of actuality and possibility. *Ash-Wednesday* is an extended contemplation of the emotional tensions of turning back to and turning away from memory and desire: 'Rose of memory / Rose of forgetfulness' (Part II). In Part I the poet haltingly tries to reconcile himself to putting things behind him:

> Because I do not hope to turn again
> Because I do not hope
> Because I do not hope to turn
> Desiring this man's gift and that man's scope
> I no longer strive to strive towards such things

The effort not to strive shows in the strangulated returnings, the beginnings-again, of the first three lines. The reconciliation is achieved in Part I with the deliberate abandonment of hope, the change from 'I do not hope' to 'I cannot hope':

'Because I cannot hope to turn again / Consequently I rejoice . . .' – although the deliberation is tautologically effortful ('Because . . . / Consequently'), too deliberate to sound quite convinced of itself. Part III gives the turning motif a Dantesque *mise-en-scène* as the poet climbs the circular stairway out of the twistings and turnings of memory, 'struggling' with the sense that each turn of experience is merely a return, that the past repeats itself not in a different, but the same pattern:

> At the first turning of the second stair
> I turned and saw below
> The same shape twisted on the banister

Turning-points, looking before and after, wear 'The deceitful face of hope and of despair', hope for what might have been and may still be, despair at how things turned out and may still turn out. But *Ash-Wednesday*'s effort of explicitly Christian renunciation is not the way of *The Waste Land*, whose expression remains intransigently ambiguous. Those half-lines ('each in his prison', 'Thinking of the key', 'each confirms a prison', 'Only at nightfall'), by looking both ways, hold the present moment, the 'always present' ('Burnt Norton' I), open to the enduring patience of indecision. The poetry embodies the sense of 'a lifetime burning in every moment' ('East Coker' V), of every moment a turning-point, as each half-line, looking grammatically backwards and forwards, acts as a new fulcrum on which the sense turns: 'the pattern is new in every moment' ('East Coker' II).

Eliot's art of deliberate and close repetition is at work in *The Waste Land*'s next lines:

> *Damyata:* The boat responded
> Gaily, to the hand expert with sail and oar
> The sea was calm, your heart would have responded
> Gaily, when invited, beating obedient
> To controlling hands

One line 'responds' to another. After two lines 'responded / Gaily' is repeated in the same enjambed form, with deliberation. The parallelism makes the variation within the repetition all the more audible. The catch in the throat comes from the catch in the variation, in the change from the past perfect, 'responded', to the apparent past conditional, 'would have responded' – apparent because the conditional should be followed by 'if', not 'when'. But 'if invited' would mean that the heart did not respond (because not invited), whereas this way of putting it ('when invited') more strongly imagines the fulfilment of desire: in the imagination the heart does respond. The speaker now realises what he did not then. The lines hauntingly enact the control (Eliot's note says that *damyata* means control) and freedom, the freedom within control, which is their subject: the imaginative release within the restraint of remembered fact. There is the freedom of the free-floating clause 'The sea was calm', neither an autonomous sentence nor a phrase, which attaches itself first, hypotactically, to the preceding phrase ('to the hand expert with sail and oar the sea was calm') and then, paratactically, to the ensuing clause ('The sea was calm' followed by a comma, and then 'your heart would have responded gaily'). In the perpetual present of the imagination the regretful freedom of memories out of control transforms into a different freedom, of memories channelled, desire patiently controlled towards a new realisation. Like 'With a little patience', 'To controlling hands' is suspended, neither ending one thing nor beginning another, neither closing one cadence nor beginning another, but intimating both, turning 'what might have been' into 'a perpetual possibility':

The Waste Land ends with an uncertain sense of an ending. The rain, several times promised, never quite arrives. The nearest it gets is in the words 'Then a damp gust / Bringing rain' (lines 393–4); but then 'the limp leaves / Waited for rain' (395–6) and 'the black clouds / Gathered far distant' (396–7); and, although the thunder speaks, at the end of the poem the plain is still arid. The poem ends still waiting upon the event, still gathering itself, still 'humped in silence'. But, again, the final verse-paragraph enacts, not failure to reach conclusion, but a resolution not to. It realises uncertainty, patiently arrived at and patiently endured. The suspension of the word 'Fishing' (line 424) between the start of the line and a caesura sounds like a determined irresolution. Does the Fisher King put the arid plain behind him as if turning his back on the poem's waste land of 'stony rubbish' and 'broken images'; or is the arid plain a backdrop to his continued fishing, as it were, for meanings? The phrase 'with the arid plain behind me' shifts grammatically from the retrospective to the prospective, from looking back to the fishing to looking forward to the setting of lands in order, from disenchantment to anticipation. 'Shall I at least set my lands in order?' is another of Eliot's patiently poker-faced, rhythmically uncommitted lines; in it hope parries with disappointment. Then the sound of this final paragraph disintegrates into irresolute verse 'fragments', not all of them in English.

Dominic Manganiello hears 'DA' as the ultimate in 'linguistic alienation': 'Even the final words of salvation are uttered enigmatically as a *fragmented* syllable, "Da" in Sanskrit, another foreign language. The voice of thunder . . . sounds like another Babylonish dialect to those locked in their own prison-house of language.'[11] As we have already registered, the prison-house of language extends to the replies which the thunder gets. Manganiello acknowledges that his account owes much to Michael Edwards, who argues that 'Babel/ Babylon is present by implication in the quotation from Psalm 137' ('By the waters of Babel I sat down and wept'), and that *The Waste Land* is partly concerned with a 'fall of language'. Edwards also notes that in Kyd's *Spanish Tragedy* Hieronymo's play, alluded to at the end of *The Waste Land*, 'enacts the fall of Babel' in a 'confusion of tongues' (Hieronymo: 'Now shall I see the fall of Babylon, / Wrought by the heav'ns in this confusion'). Edwards goes on to speculate: 'It may well have been Kyd who suggested to Eliot the possibility of a polyglot *Waste Land*, with Babel as a constituent myth.'[12] Southam intimates the self-reflexivity of *The Waste Land*'s allusion to *The Spanish Tragedy* when he writes that Hieronymo's statement, quoted in *The Waste Land*, 'Why then Ile fit you', which is his promise to write a play for the court, is 'a double-edged agreement, for he arranges that his son's murderers are themselves killed in his little play, which was made up from fragments of poetry in "sundry languages" (exactly as here in *The Waste Land*).'[13] But in fact the play 'was thought good to be set down in English more largely, for the easier understanding to every public reader', in the words of the Spanish King. The play is not, therefore, spoken in the languages Hieronymo promises, Latin, Greek, Italian and French, although we are to imagine it has been, for Hieronymo breaks in mid-play with a long monologue beginning 'Here break we off our sundry languages' to declare himself and his motives: 'know I am Hieronimo, / ... Whose tongue is tun'd to tell his latest tale.' Nor is it just the murderers of Hieronymo's son who are killed in the play: both Hieronymo himself and his son's lover commit suicide.[14] The allusion to *The Spanish Tragedy*, like so many allusions in *The Waste Land*, points in several directions, acting as an agent as much of incoherence as of coherence, even as the poetry in this last verse-paragraph displays the art of the 'fragment' with a vengeance. *The Waste Land*'s tongue is not tuned to tell its latest tale. The allusion intimates poetic self-destruction as the lines spiral into a Babylonish babble. They out-Hieronymo Hieronymo: his play may not turn out to be polyglot, but the end of *The Waste Land* does, extravagantly, to the point of self-parody. The poetry sounds as if it is aping itself, flourishing its inscrutability. Besides English, the allusive shards at the end are in Italian, Latin and French, three of the four languages Hieronymo promises; and the one from the end of *Purgatorio* XXVI, '*Poi s'ascose nel foco che gli affina*', describes the poet Arnaut Daniel 'hiding himself in the refining fire' after addressing Dante in his (Arnaut's) Provençal tongue, a fact Eliot was to mention in his essay of 1929 on Dante.[15] By contrast, the poet Eliot at the end of his poem hides behind 'a heap of broken images', which is where he began.

The 'fragments' of the heap might be put 'in order' in various ways. The nursery-rhyme refrain 'London bridge is falling down falling down falling down' may conjure up the crowd of Dantean ghosts flowing over London Bridge at the end of 'The Burial of the Dead' as well as the metropolitan destructions, with their 'falling towers', earlier in 'What the Thunder said'. In the nursery-rhyme the refrain continues 'My fair lady', which, by its absence from Eliot's allusion, may intimate the absence of fair ladies in *The Waste Land*, or possibly their fleeting presence, for example and especially in the voice of Ophelia at the end of 'A Game of Chess', whose 'sweet ladies' are the denizens of the pub. The tower is also falling down in Gérard de Nerval's sonnet, 'El Desdichado' ('The Disinherited'), of which the line '*Le Prince d'Aquitaine à la tour abolie*' becomes one of the quoted fragments, and in which, as Southam explains, 'the poet refers to himself as the disinherited Prince, heir to the tradition of the French troubadour poets who were associated with the castles of Aquitaine', and who, of course, wrote in Provençal. Moreover, 'One of the cards in the Tarot pack is the tower struck by lightning, symbolizing a lost tradition.'[16] Troubadour poetry was concerned almost exclusively with fair ladies. Arnaut Daniel suffers in Purgatory for lust, and the line about him hiding in the refining fire recalls the (Augustinian) fire of lust and expiation at the end of 'The Fire Sermon'. '*Quando fiam uti chelidon* – O swallow swallow', calls up, with the prompting of Eliot's note, *The Waste Land*'s preoccupation with the inviolable voice and the possibilities of song. This quotation from the famous 'Pervigilium Veneris' ('The Vigil of Venus') brings *The Waste Land* full circle, for the Latin poem laments the poet's inability to emulate the spring and break into song ('April is the cruellest month'), and ends by asking '*Quando fiam uti chelidon*', 'when shall I be like the swallow'. In 'Pervigilium Veneris' the swallow is Procne, sister to Philomel and wife to Tereus, who, like her sister, converts her 'complaining about a barbarous husband' into 'musical strains of love'. Eliot's note indicates that he wants his reader to make the connection with Philomel's 'inviolable voice'. Both swallow and nightingale are able to convert their pain into song.

But can the poet do so? Like the (anonymous) poet of the Latin poem, he fears poetic silence, even though this fear gets intimated at the end of the poem which is *The Waste Land*. The birds fill all the desert with inviolable voice, but he can only end by shoring fragments against his ruins, snatches of other people's poetry, a line from a nursery-rhyme, phrases from poems in sundry languages. 'Pervigilium Veneris' is a fertility song, *The Waste Land* a fertility song *manqué*.

But in all this the poet may be cocking a snook. He alludes to *The Spanish Tragedy* by recalling its sub-title, *Hieronymo is Mad Againe*, but Hieronymo's was a feigned madness. Does the end of *The Waste Land*, and other parts of it too, put on an antic disposition? Why then, he'll fit us with a poem we can make what we will of. But if the poet feels himself to be a disinherited prince of poetry like Gérard de Nerval, it is well to recall that the latter lived much of his life on the edge of sanity while composing lucid but also hallucinatorily deranged poetry.[17] Does *The Waste Land* self-destruct into fragments at its end, or does it intimate coherences yet to be achieved? Significantly, just before his suicide Hieronymo bites out his tongue so that he will not 'reveal / The thing which [he has] vow'd inviolate'.[18] Does *The Waste Land* maintain its tongue-less 'inviolable voice' to the end, uttering sounds that cannot be violated by meaning, syllables beyond comprehension? That is one way of registering the poem's final, Sanskrit, syllables.

Linguistic alienation in *The Waste Land* goes hand in hand with linguistic attraction: we are fascinated by what sounds strange. Michael Edwards, again, understands the paradox when he hears the poem's last two lines in opposed ways:

> The last words are precisely that – words:
>
> Datta. Dayadhvam. Damyata.
> Shantih shantih shantih
>
> In their utter foreignness, at once alienating and compelling, lies their significance. Salvation implies another language.... And yet the words are not entirely foreign.... Sanskrit is thought to be the oldest Indo-European language, and is therefore the root

> of all the languages in the poem. As DA is the root of the three commands. The languages scatter, to be gathered in the final words. The poem reaches back to a pre-lapsarian condition, before the dispersal of languages; and Sanskrit is its metaphor of a primitive, wise and single speech.[19]

What 'Shantih' might intimate metaphorically can only be gathered from somewhere outside the poem, from Eliot's note for instance, which originally read 'Shantih. Repeated as here, a formal ending to an Upanishad. "The Peace which passeth understanding" is a feeble translation of the content of this word'. The last phrase of this note was revised in later editions to 'is our equivalent to this word'.[20] The revision signifies Eliot's changing orientation towards Christianity. But *The Waste Land* itself became, or to the later Eliot looking back appeared to be, a step on the way to his acceptance of the Christian faith.

This later Eliot, who in the essay on Pascal elided 'religious illumination' with 'literary composition', did so again with greater deliberation twenty years later when considering 'Virgil as a Christian prophet' in his essay 'Virgil and the Christian World' (1951):

> If a prophet were by definition a man who understood the full meaning of what he was saying, this would be for me an end of the matter. But if the word 'inspiration' is to have any meaning, it must mean just this, that the speaker or writer is uttering something which he does not wholly understand – or which he may even misinterpret when the inspiration has departed from him. This is certainly true of poetic inspiration: and there is more obvious reason for admiring Isaiah as a poet than for claiming Virgil as a prophet. A poet . . . need not know what his poetry will come to mean to others; and a prophet need not understand the meaning of his prophetic utterance.[21]

This pronouncement, if applied to the authorship of *The Waste Land* – and it has the ring of personal experience – covertly sanctions a proleptic reading of the poem. 'A prophet need not understand the meaning of his prophetic utterance' can be heard as an attempt to counter the impression that *The Waste Land* is a poem of vatic riddling. But it is also relevant to recall what Eliot wrote in 'Tradition and the Individual Talent': 'Someone said: "The dead writers are remote from us because we *know* so much more than they did." Precisely, and they are that which we know.'[22] This dictum could be applied to a poet's relationship with his own past poetry. It comes down to the fact that a poet is the instrument of language, 'uttering something which he does not wholly understand'. As Eliot wrote in connection with Dante, 'the great master of language should be the great servant of it.'[23] But words 'will not stay in place, / Will not stay still' (from 'Burnt Norton' V), and every reading is therefore necessarily provisional, of its time.[24] The three 'Shantih's are an assuaging ritual of sound, possibly signifying more than they know, possibly not. They yearn perhaps for what they do not possess, the meaning which is beyond them. Their linguistic alienation realises a divorce from significant meaning, and a movement towards it. Even as they enact frustration with their unintelligibility, they placate frustration with their sound. 'Repeated as here, a formal ending': *The Waste Land*'s last words appease the need for form, they go through the motions of ending, they chant their chant. But what was composed for how it sounded came to be heard by its author, as well as by many of its readers, for how it meant, or how it could be made to mean with the friendly aid of the note.

Notes

HISTORICAL AND CULTURAL CONTEXT

1. Peter Ackroyd, *T. S. Eliot* (1984; rpt London: Sphere Books, 1985), p. 88.
2. George Plimpton (ed.), *Writers at Work: The Paris Review interviews* (Second Series, 1963; rpt Harmondsworth: Penguin, 1977), p. 110.
3. *Ibid.*, p. 99.
4. Quoted in Herbert Read, 'T. S. E. – A Memoir', in Allen Tate (ed.), *T. S. Eliot: The man and his work* (London: Chatto & Windus, 1967), p. 15.
5. To Henry Ware Eliot, 13 June 1917, *The Letters of T. S. Eliot. Vol. 1, 1898–1922*, ed. Valerie Eliot (London: Faber & Faber, 1988), p. 183.
6. 'Tradition and the individual talent' (1917), in *Selected Essays* (3rd enlarged edn, London: Faber & Faber, 1951), p. 18. To Henry Ware Eliot, 23 December 1917, *Letters*, p. 214.
7. To Mary Hutchinson, 19 September 1917, *Letters*, p. 197.
8. 'Tradition and the individual talent', in *Selected Essays*, p. 17.
9. *The Waste Land: A facsimile and transcript of the original drafts including the annotations of Ezra Pound*, ed. Valerie Eliot (London: Faber & Faber, 1971), pp. 10–13. See Ackroyd, *T. S. Eliot*, pp. 114–15.
10. 'Ode' was published only once, in the British edition of Eliot's 1920 collection of poems, *Ara Vos Prec* (London: Ovid Press), but omitted from the American edition entitled *Poems* and from all subsequent editions of Eliot's poetry. Lyndall Gordon, *Eliot's Early Years* (Oxford: Oxford UP, 1977), p. 75.

11. Text and translation from Francis Scarfe (ed.), *Baudelaire* (Harmondsworth: Penguin, 1961), p. 193.
12. A. D. Moody, *Thomas Stearns Eliot: Poet* (Cambridge: Cambridge UP, 1979), pp. 38, 39.
13. Eliot's thesis was eventually published as *Knowledge and Experience in the Philosophy of F. H. Bradley* (London: Faber & Faber, 1964).
14. Ackroyd, *T. S. Eliot*, pp. 50, 69, 70.
15. 'Tradition and the individual talent', in *Selected Essays*, pp. 18–19.
16. 'A brief introduction to the method of Paul Valéry', in Paul Valéry, *Le Serpent*, trans. Mark Wardle (London: R. Cobden-Sanderson for *The Criterion*, 1924), p. 12.
17. *The Waste Land: A facsimile and transcript*, pp. 90–7, 112–13, and note on p. 130.
18. These words are by Eliot about Pascal: 'The "Pensées" of Pascal' (1931), in *Selected Essays*, p. 405. Eliot said he was describing his own experience of writing 'What the Thunder said'. See *The Waste Land: A facsimile and transcript*, note on p. 129.
19. 'Caesarian Operation' is Pound's phrase in some lines of doggerel he wrote for Eliot about his part in the composition of *The Waste Land*. See *Selected Letters of Ezra Pound*, ed. D. D. Paige (1950; rpt New York: New Directions, 1971), p. 170.
20. *Writers at Work*, p. 96.
21. *The Waste Land: A facsimile and transcript*, *passim*.
22. Ackroyd, *T. S. Eliot*, p. 117.
23. Donald Davie, *Under Briggflatts: A history of poetry in Great Britain 1960–1988* (Manchester: Carcanet, 1989), p. 100.
24. See Ackroyd, *T. S. Eliot*, p. 126.

CRITICAL RECEPTION

1. Clive Bell, 'Plus de Jazz', *The New Republic* **28** (21 September 1921), rpt in Michael Grant (ed.), *T. S. Eliot: The critical heritage*, vol. 1 (London: Routledge & Kegan Paul, 1982), p. 118.
2. Stephen Spender, 'Diary', *London Review of Books* **14** (7) (9 April 1992), p. 25.
3. *The Waste Land: A facsimile and transcript of the original drafts including the annotations of Ezra Pound*, ed. Valerie Eliot (London: Faber & Faber, 1971), p. 1.

4. Important here is Donald Davie, 'Pound and Eliot: A distinction' (1970), in *The Poet in the Imaginary Museum: Essays of two decades*, ed. Barry Alpert (Manchester: Carcanet, 1977), pp. 191–207.
5. See the title of Hugh Kenner's book, *The Invisible Poet: T. S. Eliot* (1960; rpt London: Methuen, 1965).
6. Seamus Heaney, *The Government of the Tongue: The 1986 T. S. Eliot memorial lectures and other critical writings* (London and Boston: Faber & Faber, 1988), p. 92.
7. Ted Hughes, *A Dancer to God: Tributes to T. S. Eliot* (London and Boston: Faber & Faber, 1992).
8. Edgell Rickword, 'The Modern Poet', *Calendar of Modern Letters* **2** (December 1925); rpt in Grant (ed.), *T. S. Eliot: The critical heritage*, vol. 1, p. 219.
9. Conrad Aiken, 'An Anatomy of Melancholy', *The New Republic* **33** (7 February 1923); rpt in Allen Tate (ed.), *T. S. Eliot: The man and his work* (London: Chatto & Windus, 1967), p. 202.
10. Laura Riding and Robert Graves, *A Survey of Modernist Poetry* (1927; rpt London: Heinemann, 1929), p. 51.
11. John Crowe Ransom, 'Waste Lands', *New York Evening Post Literary Review* **3** (14 July 1923); rpt in Grant (ed.), *T. S. Eliot: The critical heritage*, vol. 1, p. 177.
12. Allen Tate, 'A reply to Ransom', *New York Evening Post Literary Review* **3** (4 August 1923); rpt in Grant (ed.) *T. S. Eliot: The critical heritage*, vol. 1, p. 182.
13. Michael Grant, 'Introduction', *T. S. Eliot: The critical heritage*, vol. 1, p. 21.
14. F.R. Leavis, *New Bearings in English Poetry: A study of the contemporary situation* (1932; rpt Harmondsworth: Penguin, 1967), pp. 81, 87.
15. Kenner, *The Invisible Poet: T. S. Eliot*, p. 128.
16. I.A. Richards, 'Mr. Eliot's Poems', *New Statesman* **26** (20 February 1926); rpt in Grant (ed.), *T. S. Eliot: The critical heritage*, vol. 1, p. 238. This review appeared as an appendix in the 1926 reissue of Richards' *Principles of Literary Criticism*.
17. Edmund Wilson, 'Stravinsky and others', *The New Republic* **46** (10 March 1926); rpt in Grant (ed.), *T. S. Eliot: The critical heritage*, vol. 1, p. 239.
18. Edgell Rickword, 'A Fragmentary Poem', unsigned review, *Times Literary Supplement* **1131** (20 September 1923); rpt in Grant (ed.), *T. S. Eliot: The critical heritage*, vol. 1, p. 185.
19. 'Ulysses, order, and myth', *The Dial* (November 1923); rpt in *Selected Prose of T. S. Eliot*, ed. Frank Kermode (London: Faber & Faber, 1975), p. 177.

20. Robert L. Schwarz, *Broken Images: A study of The Waste Land* (Lewisburg, PA: Bucknell UP; London and Toronto: Associated University Presses, 1988), p. 14. The most recent and extensive survey of Eliot's knowlege of anthropology is Robert Crawford, *The Savage and the City in the work of T. S. Eliot* (Oxford: Oxford UP, 1987); while this is very informative about where Eliot's earlier poetry, including *The Waste Land*, came from, its approach is in danger of substituting sources for the work.
21. Helen Gardner, *The Art of T. S. Eliot* (London: Cresset Press, 1949).
22. Lyndall Gordon, *Eliot's Early Years* (Oxford: Oxford UP, 1977), p. 2.
23. Eloise Knapp Hay, *T. S. Eliot's Negative Way* (Cambridge, MA: Harvard UP, 1982).

THEORETICAL PERSPECTIVES

1. Frank Kermode, 'A Babylonish dialect', in Allen Tate (ed.), *T. S. Eliot: The man and his work* (London: Chatto & Windus, 1967), p. 239.
2. See Wolfgang Iser, *The Act of Reading: A theory of aesthetic response* (London and Henley: Routledge & Kegan Paul, 1978).
3. Steve Ellis, '*The Waste Land* and the reader's response', in Tony Davies and Nigel Wood (eds), *The Waste Land* (Buckingham: Open University Press, 1994).
4. Mick Burton, in David Murray (ed.), *Literary Theory and Poetry: Extending the canon* (London and Braintree: Batsford, 1989).
5. Raman Selden, *Practising Theory and Reading Literature* (Hemel Hempstead: Harvester Wheatsheaf, 1989), pp. 127–8. See Hans-Georg Gadamer, *Truth and Method*, trans. Garrett Barden and John Cumming (London: Sheed & Ward, 1975).
6. Marianne Thormählen, *The Waste Land: A fragmentary wholeness* (Lund: C. W. K. Gleerup, 1978), pp. 206, 205. See J. Hillis Miller, *Poets of Reality: Six twentieth-century writers* (Cambridge, MA: Harvard UP, 1965).
7. Jewel Spears Brooker and Joseph Bentley, *Reading The Waste Land: Modernism and the limits of interpretation* (Amherst, MA: University of Massachusetts Press, 1990), pp. 6, 8, 6, 4.
8. *Ibid.*, p. 6.
9. Both essays by Davie reprinted in *The Poet in the Imaginary*

Museum: Essays of two decades, ed. Barry Alpert (Manchester: Carcanet, 1977), pp. 117–21, 191–207.
10. Michael Grant, 'Introduction', *T. S. Eliot: The critical heritage*, vol. 1 (London: Routledge & Kegan Paul, 1982), p. 54.
11. Denis Donoghue, 'The word within a word', in A. D. Moody (ed.), *The Waste Land in Different Voices* (London: Edward Arnold, 1974), p. 201.
12. 'A brief introduction to the method of Paul Valéry', in Paul Valéry, *Le Serpent*, trans. Mark Wardle (London: R. Cobden-Sanderson for *The Criterion*, 1924), p. 12.
13. 'From Poe to Valéry' (1948), in *To Criticize the Critic* (London: Faber & Faber, 1965), p. 39.
14. Brooker and Bentley, *Reading The Waste Land*, pp. 6, 8.
15. 'A brief introduction to the method of Paul Valéry', p. 12.
16. 'Tradition and the individual talent' (1917), in *Selected Essays* (3rd enlarged edn, London: Faber & Faber, 1951), p. 21.
17. Maud Ellmann, *The Poetics of Impersonality: T. S. Eliot and Ezra Pound* (Brighton: Harvester Press, 1987), pp. 38–41.
18. Davie, 'Mr Eliot' (1963), in *The Poet in the Imaginary Museum*, p. 119.
19. Ellmann, *The Poetics of Impersonality*, p. 92.
20. Davie, 'Pound and Eliot: A distinction' (1970), in *The Poet in the Imaginary Museum*, p. 204.
21. 'Virgil and the Christian world' (1951), in *On Poetry and Poets* (London: Faber & Faber, 1957), p. 122.
22. Donoghue, 'The word within a word', in Moody (ed.), *The Waste Land in Different Voices*, pp. 194, 196.
23. 'What is minor poetry?' (1944), in *On Poetry and Poets*, p. 52. Christopher Ricks, *T. S. Eliot and Prejudice* (London and Boston: Faber & Faber, 1988), p. 282.
24. In this connection see Tony Pinkney's difficult but convincing Kleinian psychoanalytic reading, *Women in the Poetry of T. S. Eliot: A psychoanalytic approach* (London and Basingstoke: Macmillan, 1984).
25. *The Waste Land: A facsimile and transcript of the original drafts including the annotations of Ezra Pound*, ed. Valerie Eliot (London: Faber & Faber, 1971), pp. 22, 23, 26, 27, 38, 39, 40, 41.
26. See Ricks, *T. S. Eliot and Prejudice*, p. 39, for a compelling discussion of this matter.
27. See *The Waste Land: A facsimile and transcript*, note on p. 127.
28. *Ibid.*, p. 3.
29. Joseph Conrad, *Heart of Darkness* (1902; New York: Norton, 1971), pp. 28, 48, 49, 50, 78.

I. 'THE BURIAL OF THE DEAD'

1. 'From Poe to Valéry', in *To Criticize the Critic* (London: Faber & Faber, 1965), p. 39.
2. See Christopher Ricks, *T. S. Eliot and Prejudice* (London and Boston: Faber & Faber, 1988), pp. 175–6. Ricks convincingly argues against the contention often made 'that the opening lines of the General Prologue to the *Canterbury Tales* settle the matter'.
3. *Poetry*, March 1913: usefully reproduced in Peter Jones (ed.), *Imagist Poetry* (Harmondsworth: Penguin, 1972), pp. 130–4. See also Eliot's retrospective statement, informative in its evasiveness: 'The *point de repère* usually and conveniently taken as the starting point of modern poetry is the group denominated "imagists" in London about 1910.' ('American Literature and the American Language' [1953], in *To Criticize the Critic*.)
4. 'The perfect critic', in *The Sacred Wood* (1920; 2nd edn, London: Methuen, 1928), p. 8.
5. For a recent and compelling elaboration of this idea, see Michael Edwards, 'Rewriting *The Waste Land*', in David Jasper and Colin Crowder (eds), *European Literature and Theology in the Twentieth Century: Ends of time* (London and Basingstoke: Macmillan, 1990), pp. 70–85.
6. *The Waste Land: A facsimile and transcript of the original drafts inlcuding the annotations of Ezra Pound*, ed. Valerie Eliot (London: Faber & Faber, 1971), pp. 6, 7.
7. Jones (ed.), *Imagist Poetry*, p. 131.
8. B. C. Southam, *A Student's Guide to the Selected Poems of T. S. Eliot* (1st edn, New York: Harcourt Brace and World, 1969), p. 73.
9. See Hugh Kenner, *The Invisible Poet: T. S. Eliot* (1960; rpt London: Methuen, 1965), p. 136.
10. 'From Poe to Valéry', in *To Criticize the Critic*, p. 39.
11. Michael Edwards, *Towards a Christian Poetics* (London and Basingstoke: Macmillan, 1984), p. 108.
12. Conrad Aiken, 'An anatomy of melancholy', in Allen Tate (ed.), *T. S. Eliot: The man and his work* (London: Chatto & Windus, 1967), p. 195.
13. See *The Waste Land: A facsimile and transcript*, pp. 94, 95, and note on p. 129.
14. Ricks, *T. S. Eliot and Prejudice*, pp. 152, 153.
15. For example in 'What the Thunder said': 'By this, and this only, we have existed' equivocates, as I argue later. And 'only'

equivocates in other poems by Eliot, in 'The Hollow Men', for instance, where the lines 'The hope only / Of empty men' are Janus-faced.

16. Grover Smith, *T. S. Eliot's Poetry and Plays: A study in sources and meaning* (1956, 2nd edn, Chicago: University of Chicago Press, 1974), p. 76.
17. See Kenner, *The Invisible Poet*, pp. 138–40.
18. Edwards, *Towards a Christian Poetics*, pp. 108–9.
19. Kenner, for instance, writes simply that the hyacinth girl 'speaks with urgent hurt simplicity, like the mad Ophelia' (*The Invisible Poet*, p. 138).
20. See Smith, *T. S. Eliot's Poetry and Plays*, p. 76.
21. Ricks, *T. S. Eliot and Prejudice*, p. 186.
22. John Lennard, *But I Digress: The exploitation of parentheses in English printed verse* (Oxford: Oxford UP, 1991), p. 190.
23. Ricks, *T. S. Eliot and Prejudice*, p. 186.
24. Kenner, *The Invisible Poet*, p. 49.
25. *The Waste Land: A facsimile and transcript*, pp. 8, 9.
26. *Ibid.*, pp. 30, 31, 42, 43.
27. Text and translation from Francis Scarfe (ed.), *Baudelaire* (Harmondsworth: Penguin, 1961), p. 156.
28. Eliot, 'Introduction' to Paul Valéry, *The Art of Poetry*, trans. Denise Folliot (London: Routledge, 1958), p. xi.
29. 'Baudelaire' (1930), in *Selected Essays* (3rd enlarged edn, London: Faber & Faber, 1951), p. 423.

II. 'A GAME OF CHESS'

1. *Antony and Cleopatra*, II. ii. 199.
2. See Donald Davie, 'The relation between syntax and music in some modern poems in English' (1961), in *The Poet in the Imaginary Museum: Essays of two decades*, ed. Barry Alpert (Manchester: Carcanet, 1977), p. 101.
3. John Lennard, *But I Digress: The exploitation of parentheses in English printed verse* (Oxford: Oxford UP, 1991), p. 192.
4. B. C. Southam, *A Student's Guide to the Selected Poems of T. S. Eliot* (1st edn, New York: Harcourt Brace and World, 1969), pp. 78–9.
5. *The Waste Land: A facsimile and transcript of the original drafts including the annotations of Ezra Pound*, ed. Valerie Eliot (London: Faber & Faber, 1971), pp. 10, 11, 16, 17.
6. *Ibid.*

7. Michael Edwards, *Towards a Christian Poetics* (London and Basingstoke: Macmillan, 1984), p. 110.
8. *Hamlet*, IV. v. 73. See also Ophelia's songs in IV. v.

III. 'THE FIRE SERMON'

1. See 'Andrew Marvell' (1921), in *Selected Essays* (3rd enlarged edn, London: Faber & Faber, 1951), pp. 295–6.
2. B. C. Southam, *A Student's Guide to the Selected Poems of T. S. Eliot* (1st edn, New York: Harcourt Brace and World, 1969), p. 80.
3. Grover Smith, *T. S. Eliot's Poetry and Plays: A study in sources and meaning* (1956; 2nd edn, Chicago, IL: University of Chicago Press, 1974), p. 85. *The Tempest*, I. ii. 388.
4. Stefan Hawlin, 'Eliot reads *The Waste Land*: Text and recording', *Modern Language Review* 87 (July 1992), pp. 548–9.
5. See Smith, *T. S. Eliot's Poetry and Plays*, p. 86.
6. Southam, *A Student's Guide*, p. 82.
7. *Ibid.*
8. *Ibid.*
9. See *The Waste Land: A facsimile and transcript of the original drafts including the annotations of Ezra Pound*, ed. Valerie Eliot (London: Faber & Faber, 1971), pp. 30, 31, 36, 37, 42, 43. The word 'only' does not appear in one of the three versions of the excised line which I quote; and Eliot has deleted from two of the three versions of the excised passage the other two lines I quote, possibly before Pound struck through the whole passage.
10. Hugh Kenner, 'The Urban Apocalypse', in A. Walton Litz (ed.), *Eliot in His Time: Essays on the occasion of the fiftieth anniversary of The Waste Land* (Princeton, NJ, and London: Princeton UP and Oxford UP, 1973), p. 28. For a fuller discussion of this excised passage and Kenner's views, see my *T. S. Eliot: A Virgilian poet* (London and Basingstoke: Macmillan, 1989), pp. 37–9. This paragraph draws on that discussion.
11. Hugh Kenner, *The Invisible Poet: T. S. Eliot* (1960; rpt London: Methuen, 1965), pp. 35, 36, 128.
12. *The Waste Land: A facsimile and transcript*, pp. 30, 31, 42, 43.
13. *Ibid.*
14. 'Eliot was not . . . averse to deliberate, immediate repetitions but was sensitive to later and accidental occurrences of a word.' Helen Gardner, *The Composition of Four Quartets* (London: Faber & Faber, 1978), p. 165.

15. See Donald Davie, 'Mr Eliot' (1963), in *The Poet in the Imaginary Museum: Essays of two decades*, ed. Barry Alpert (Manchester: Carcanet, 1977), p. 120. However, Davie does not consider the possibility of hearing 'can see' as an intransitive verb, but wants to make 'the evening hour' what Tiresias sees.
16. *The Waste Land: A facsimile and transcript*, pp. 34, 35, 46, 47.
17. Christopher Ricks, *T. S. Eliot and Prejudice* (London and Boston: Faber & Faber, 1988), p. 257.
18. 'Musical interplay' is Hawlin's phrase ('Eliot reads *The Waste Land*: Text and recording', p. 550).
19. *Ibid.*, p. 548.
20. *Ibid.*, p. 551.
21. St Augustine, *Confessions*, III. i.
22. *Ibid.*, X. 34; Amos 4: 11; Zechariah 3: 2. See also Smith, *T. S. Eliot's Poetry and Plays*, p. 90; Southam, *A Student's Guide*, p. 87.

IV. 'DEATH BY WATER'

1. *The Waste Land: A facsimile and transcript of the original drafts including the annotations of Ezra Pound*, ed. Valerie Eliot (London: Faber & Faber, 1971), pp. 54–69. George Plimpton (ed.), *Writers at Work: The Paris Review Interviews* (Second Series, 1963; rpt Harmondsworth: Penguin, 1977), p. 96. 'Dante' (1929), in *Selected Essays* (3rd enarged edn, London: Faber & Faber, 1951), p. 250.
2. *The Divine Comedy of Dante Alighieri*, trans. John D. Sinclair (3 vols, 1939; rpt New York: Oxford UP, 1972–4), *Inferno*, note to Canto XXVI, p. 332.
3. *The Waste Land: A facsimile and transcript*, pp. 60, 61, 68, 69. This paragraph draws on my *T. S. Eliot: A Virgilian poet* (London and Basingstoke: Macmillan, 1989), pp. 129–31 *passim.*
4. William Arrowsmith, 'Daedal harmonies: A dialogue on Eliot and the Classics', *Southern Review* **13** (Winter 1977), pp. 35, 36.

V. 'WHAT THE THUNDER SAID'

1. Letter to Peter Russell, 19 May 1948, quoted in *The Waste

Land: A facsimile and transcript of the original drafts including the annotations of Ezra Pound, ed. Valerie Eliot (London: Faber & Faber, 1971), p. 129.

2. 'The "Pensées" of Pascal' (1931), in *Selected Essays* (3rd enlarged edn, London: Faber & Faber, 1951), p. 405. See *The Waste Land: A facsimile and transcript*, p. 129.
3. Christopher Ricks, *T. S. Eliot and Prejudice* (London and Boston: Faber & Faber, 1988), pp. 178–9.
4. See two letters to Ford Madox Ford, 14 August 1923 and 4 October 1923, quoted in *The Waste Land: A facsimile and transcript*, p. 129. Ricks, *T. S. Eliot and Prejudice*, p. 180.
5. C. K. Stead, *Pound, Yeats, Eliot and the Modernist Movement* (London and Basingstoke: Macmillan, 1986), p. 114.
6. The three previous citations are from *Ibid.*, pp. 115–16.
7. *Ibid.*, p. 115.
8. F. R. Leavis, *New Bearings in English Poetry: A study of the contemporary situation* (1932; rpt Harmondsworth: Penguin, 1967), p. 86.
9. Stead, *Pound, Yeats, Eliot*, p. 116.
10. This and the previous paragraph draw on my *T. S. Eliot: A Virgilian poet* (London and Basingstoke: Macmillan, 1989), pp. 54–5.
11. Dominic Manganiello, *T. S. Eliot and Dante* (London and Basingstoke: Macmillan, 1989), pp. 54, 55.
12. Michael Edwards, *Towards a Christian Poetics* (London and Basingstoke: Macmillan, 1984), pp. 111–12. *The Spanish Tragedy*, IV. i. 190–1.
13. Southam, *A Student's Guide*, pp. 92–3. *The Spanish Tragedy*, IV. i. 68; IV. iv. 268, 331.
14. *The Spanish Tragedy*, IV. iv. 268; IV. i. 171–2; IV. iv. 331, 340–2; IV. iv *passim*.
15. 'Dante' (1929), in *Selected Essays*, p. 256.
16. Southam, *A Student's Guide*, p. 92.
17. See especially de Nerval's *Aurélia*.
18. *The Spanish Tragedy*, IV. iv. 459–60.
19. Edwards, *Towards a Christian Poetics*, p. 113.
20. See the text of the first edition of *The Waste Land* (New York: Boni and Liveright, 1922) rpt in *The Waste Land: A facsimile and transcript*, p. 149.
21. 'Virgil and the Christian world', in *On Poetry and Poets* (London: Faber & Faber, 1957), pp. 122–3.
22. 'Tradition and the individual talent' (1917), in *Selected Essays*, p. 16.

23. 'What Dante means to me', in *To Criticize the Critic* (London: Faber & Faber, 1965), p. 133.
24. This argument draws on my *T. S. Eliot: A Virgilian poet*, pp. 161–2.

Select Bibliography

WORKS BY T. S. ELIOT

Poetry

Collected Poems 1909–1962 (London: Faber & Faber, 1963).

The Waste Land: A facsimile and transcript of the original drafts including the annotations of Ezra Pound, ed. Valerie Eliot (London: Faber & Faber, 1971).

Prose

'A brief introduction to the method of Paul Valéry', in Paul Valéry, *Le Serpent*, trans. Mark Wardle (London: R. Cobden-Sanderson for *The Criterion*, 1924).

Knowledge and Experience in the Philosophy of F. H. Bradley (London: Faber and Faber, 1964).

The Letters of T. S. Eliot. Vol. I, 1898–1922, ed. Valerie Eliot (London: Faber & Faber, 1988).

On Poetry and Poets (London: Faber & Faber, 1957).

The Sacred Wood (1920; 2nd edn, London: Methuen, 1928).

Selected Essays (3rd enlarged edn, London: Faber & Faber, 1951).

Selected Prose of T. S. Eliot, ed. Frank Kermode (London: Faber & Faber, 1975).

To Criticize the Critic (London: Faber & Faber, 1965).

The Use of Poetry and the Use of Criticism (London: Faber & Faber, 1933).

BIBLIOGRAPHIES

Gallup, Donald, *T. S. Eliot: A bibliography* (2nd edn, London: Faber & Faber, 1969).

Knowles, Sebastian D. G. and Leonard, Scott A. (eds), *T. S. Eliot: Man and poet. Vol. Two: Annotated Bibliography of Eliot Criticism 1977–86* (Orono: National Poetry Foundation, University of Maine, 1990).

Martin, Mildred, *A Half-Century of Eliot Criticism: An annotated bibliography of books and articles in English, 1916–1965* (Lewisburg, PA: Bucknell UP, 1972).

Ricks, Beatrice, *T. S. Eliot: A bibliography of secondary works* (Scarecrow Author Bibliographies, No. 45, Metuchen, NJ: Scarecrow Press, 1980).

BIOGRAPHICAL

Ackroyd, Peter, *T. S. Eliot* (1984; rpt London: Sphere Books, 1985).

Chiari, Joseph, *T. S. Eliot: A memoir* (London: Enitharmon Press, 1982).

Gordon, Lyndall, *Eliot's Early Years* (Oxford: Oxford UP, 1977).

Howarth, Herbert, *Notes on Some Figures behind T. S. Eliot* (London: Chatto & Windus, 1965).

Matthews, T. S., *Great Tom: Notes towards the definition of T. S. Eliot* (London: Weidenfeld & Nicolson, 1974).

Sencourt, Robert, *T. S. Eliot: A memoir*, ed. Donald Adamson (London: Garnstone Press, 1971).

Sharpe, Tony, *T. S. Eliot: A literary life* (London and Basingstoke: Macmillan, 1991).

CRITICAL WORKS

Single-author books on Eliot

Bergonzi, Bernard, *T. S. Eliot* (London and Basingstoke: Macmillan, 1972).

Calder, Angus, *T. S. Eliot* (Brighton: Harvester Press, 1987).

Crawford, Robert, *The Savage and the City in the work of T. S. Eliot* (Oxford, Oxford UP, 1987).

Drew, Elizabeth, *T. S. Eliot: The design of his poetry* (London: Eyre & Spottiswoode, 1950).

Frye, Northrop, *T. S. Eliot* (Edinburgh: Oliver & Boyd, 1963).

Gardner, Helen, *The Art of T. S. Eliot* (1949; rpt London: Faber & Faber, 1968).

Gray, Piers, *T. S. Eliot's Intellectual and Poetic Development, 1909–1922* (Brighton: Harvester Press, 1982).

Hay, Eloise Knapp, *T. S. Eliot's Negative Way* (Cambridge, MA: Harvard UP, 1982).

Hughes, Ted, *A Dancer to God: Tributes to T. S. Eliot* (London: Faber & Faber, 1992).

Kenner, Hugh, *The Invisible Poet: T. S. Eliot* (1960; rpt London: Methuen, 1965).

Manganiello, Dominic, *T. S. Eliot and Dante* (London and Basingstoke: Macmillan, 1989).

Matthiessen, F. O., *The Achievement of T. S. Eliot: An essay on the nature of poetry* (1935; 2nd rev. edn, London and New York: Oxford UP, 1947).

Maxwell, D. E. S., *The Poetry of T. S. Eliot* (London: Routledge & Kegan Paul, 1952).

Moody, A. D., *Thomas Stearns Eliot: Poet* (Cambridge: Cambridge UP, 1979).

Patterson, Gertrude, *T. S. Eliot: Poems in the making* (Manchester: Manchester UP, 1971).

Pinkney, Tony, *Women in the Poetry of T. S. Eliot: A psychoanalytic approach* (London and Basingstoke: Macmillan, 1984).

Reeves, Gareth, *T. S. Eliot: A Virgilian poet* (London and Basingstoke: Macmillan, 1989).

Ricks, Christopher, *T. S. Eliot and Prejudice* (London and Boston: Faber & Faber, 1988).

Riquelme, John Paul, *Harmony and Dissonances: T. S. Eliot, Romanticism and imagination* (Baltimore, MD, and London: Johns Hopkins UP, 1991).

Schneider, Elisabeth, *T. S. Eliot: The pattern in the carpet* (Berkeley: University of California Press, 1975).

Scofield, Martin, *T. S. Eliot: The poems* (Cambridge: Cambridge UP, 1988).

Skaff, William, *The Philosophy of T. S. Eliot: From skepticism to a Surrealist poetic 1909–1927* (Philadelphia: University of Pennsylvania Press, 1986).

Smidt, Kristian, *Poetry and Belief in the Work of T. S. Eliot* (London: Routledge & Kegan Paul, 1961).

Smith, Grover, *T. S. Eliot's Poetry and Plays: A study in sources and meaning* (1956; 2nd edn, Chicago: University of Chicago Press, 1974).

Southam, B. C., *A Student's Guide to the Selected Poems of T. S. Eliot* (1st edn, New York: Harcourt Brace and World, 1969).

Spender, Stephen, *T. S. Eliot*, Fontana Modern Masters (London: Fontana, 1975).

Traversi, Derek, *T. S. Eliot: The longer poems* (London: Bodley Head, 1976).

Unger, Leonard, *T. S. Eliot: Moments and patterns* (Minneapolis: Minnesota UP, 1966).

Ward, David, *T. S. Eliot: Between Two Worlds: A reading of T. S. Eliot's poetry and plays* (London and Boston: Routledge & Kegan Paul, 1973).

Williamson, George, *A Reader's Guide to T. S. Eliot* (1955; rpt London: Thames & Hudson, 1962).

Books and articles on The Waste Land

Bedient, Calvin, *He Do the Police in Different Voices: The Waste Land and its protagonist* (Chicago: Chicago UP, 1986).

Bradbrook, M. C., *T. S. Eliot: The making of The Waste Land* (Harlow, Longman for the British Council, 1972).

Brooker, Jewel Spears and Bentley, Joseph, *Reading The Waste Land: Modernism and the limits of interpretation* (Amherst: University of Massachusetts Press, 1990).

Brooks, Cleanth, '*The Waste Land*: An analysis', in *Modern Poetry and the Tradition* (Chapel Hill: University of North Carolina Press, 1939); rpt in B. Rajan (ed.), *T. S. Eliot: A study of his writings by several hands* (London: Dennis Dobson, 1947), pp. 7–36.

Cox, C. B. and Hinchcliffe, A. P. (eds), *The Waste Land: A casebook* (London: Macmillan, 1968).

Davie, Donald, 'The relation between syntax and music in some modern poems in English' (1961), 'Mr Eliot' (1963), 'Pound and Eliot: A distinction' (1970), in *The Poet in the Imaginary Museum: Essays of two decades*, ed. Barry Alpert (Manchester: Carcanet, 1977), pp. 93–103, 117–21, 191–207.

Davie, Donald, '*The Waste Land* drafts and transcripts', in *Under Briggflatts: A history of poetry in Great Britain 1960–1988* (Manchester: Carcanet, 1989), pp. 98–102.

Davies, Tony and Wood, Nigel (eds), *The Waste Land* (Buckingham: Open University Press, 1994).

Edwards, Michael, 'Rewriting *The Waste Land*', in David Jasper and Colin Crowder (eds), *European Literature and Theology in the Twentieth Century: Ends of time* (London and Basingstoke: Macmillan, 1990).

Everett, Barbara, 'Eliot in and out of *The Waste Land*', *Critical Quarterly* **17** (Spring 1975), pp. 7–30.
Hawlin, Stefan, 'Eliot reads *The Waste Land*: Text and recording', *Modern Language Review* **87** (July 1992), pp. 545–54.
Kelly, Lionel, ' "What are the roots that clutch?": Eliot's *The Waste Land* and Frazer's *The Golden Bough*', in Robert Fraser (ed.), *Sir James Frazer and the Literary Imagination: Essays in affinity and influence* (London and Basingstoke: Macmillan, 1990), pp. 192–206.
Litz, A. Walton (ed.), *Eliot in his Time: Essays on the occasion of the fiftieth anniversary of* The Waste Land (Princeton, NJ, and London: Princeton UP and Oxford UP, 1973).
Martin, Jay (ed.), *T. S. Eliot's* The Waste Land*: A collection of critical essays* (Englewood Cliffs, NJ: Prentice Hall, 1968).
Medcalf, Stephen, 'T. S. Eliot's *Metamorphoses*: Ovid and *The Waste Land*', in Charles Martindale (ed.), *Ovid Renewed: Ovidian influences on literature and art from the Middle Ages to the twentieth century* (Cambridge: Cambridge UP, 1988), pp. 233–46.
Moody, A. D. (ed.), *The Waste Land in Different Voices* (London: Edward Arnold, 1974).
Schwarz, Robert L., *Broken Images: A study of* The Waste Land (Lewisburg, PA: Bucknell UP; London and Toronto: Associated University Presses, 1988).
Smith, Grover, *The Waste Land* (London: George Allen & Unwin, 1983).
Thormählen, Marianne, *The Waste Land: A fragmentary wholeness* (Lund: C. W. K. Gleerup, 1978).

Collections of essays on Eliot

Bagchee, Shyamal (ed.), *T. S. Eliot: A voice descanting* (London and Basingstoke: Macmillan, 1990).
Braybrooke, Neville (ed.), *T. S. Eliot: A symposium for his seventieth birthday* (London: Rupert Hart-Davis, 1958).
Bush, Ronald (ed.), *T. S. Eliot: The modernist in history* (Cambridge: Cambridge UP, 1991).
Clarke, Graham (ed.), *T. S. Eliot: Critical assessments* (4 vols, London: Helm, 1990).
Cowan, Laura (ed.), *T. S. Eliot: Man and poet. Vol. One* (Orono: National Poetry Foundation, University of Maine, 1990).
Grant, Michael (ed.), *T. S. Eliot: The critical heritage* (2 vols, London: Routledge & Kegan Paul, 1982).

Kenner, Hugh (ed.), *T. S. Eliot: A collection of critical essays* (Englewood Cliffs, NJ: Prentice Hall, 1962).
March, Richard and Tambimuttu (eds), *T. S. Eliot: A symposium* (London: Editions Poetry London, 1948).
Martin, Graham (ed.), *Eliot in Perspective: A symposium* (London: Macmillan, 1970).
Tate, Allen (ed.), *T. S. Eliot: The man and his work* (London: Chatto & Windus, 1967).

Books containing commentary on Eliot and on The Waste Land

Ackroyd, Peter, *Notes for a New Culture* (London: Vision Press, 1976).
Alvarez, A., *The Shaping Spirit* (London: Chatto & Windus, 1958).
Edwards, Michael, *Towards a Christian Poetics* (London and Basingstoke: Macmillan, 1984).
Ellmann, Maud, *The Poetics of Impersonality: T. S. Eliot and Ezra Pound* (Brighton: Harvester Press, 1987).
Gelpi, Albert, *A Coherent Splendor: The American poetic renaissance 1910–1950* (Cambridge: Cambridge UP, 1988).
Harding, D. W., *Experience into Words* (1963; rpt Harmondsworth: Penguin, 1974).
Heaney, Seamus, *The Government of the Tongue: The 1986 T. S. Eliot memorial lectures and other critical writings* (London and Boston: Faber & Faber, 1988).
Kenner, Hugh, *The Pound Era* (Berkeley and Los Angeles: University of California Press, 1971).
Leavis, F. R., *New Bearings in English Poetry: A study of the contemporary situation* (1932; rpt Harmondsworth: Penguin, 1967).
Lennard, John, *But I Digress: The exploitation of parentheses in English printed verse* (Oxford: Oxford UP, 1991).
McDiarmid, Lucy, *Saving Civilization: Yeats, Eliot and Auden between the wars* (Cambridge: Cambridge UP, 1984).
Miller, J. Hillis, *Poets of Reality: Six twentieth-century writers* (Cambridge, MA: Harvard UP, 1965).
Riding, Laura and Graves, Robert, *A Survey of Modernist Poetry* (1927; rpt London: Heinemann, 1929).
Stead, C. K., *The New Poetic: Yeats to Eliot* (London: Hutchinson, 1964).
Stead, C. K., *Pound, Yeats, Eliot and the Modernist Movement* (London and Basingstoke: Macmillan, 1986).

Svarny, Erik, *'The Men of 1914': T. S. Eliot and early modernism* (Milton Keynes: Open University Press, 1988).
Wilson, Edmund, *Axel's Castle: A study in the imaginative literature of 1890–1930* (1931; rpt London: Fontana, 1961).

OTHER WORKS OF INTEREST

Arrowsmith, William, 'Daedal harmonies: A dialogue on Eliot and the Classics', *Southern Review* **13** (Winter 1977), pp. 1–47.
Gadamer, Hans-Georg, *Truth and Method*, trans. Garrett Barden and John Cumming (London: Sheed & Ward, 1975).
Iser, Wolfgang, *The Act of Reading: A theory of aesthetic response* (London and Henley: Routledge & Kegan Paul, 1978).
Jones, Peter (ed.), *Imagist Poetry* (Harmondsworth: Penguin, 1972).
Plimpton, George (ed.), *Writers at Work: The Paris Review interviews* (Second Series, 1963; rpt Harmondsworth: Penguin, 1977).

Index